Gerald Priestland, writer and broad[...] for such programmes as 'Priestland'[...] on which he contributed many a thou[...] the day. He was the BBC's correspondent in Washington before becoming Religious Affairs Correspondent until his retirement. He died in 1991. Sylvia Priestland, his widow, lives in London and near Penzance.

All the photographs in this book
were taken by Sylvia Priestland

By Gerald Priestland

GERALD AND SYLVIA
PRIESTLAND

Priestlands'
Cornwall

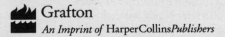
Grafton
An Imprint of HarperCollins*Publishers*

To the children
Jennet, Andreas, Oliver and Diana
whom we brought to Zennor
and who stayed to love it
(especially Diana who lives nearby
to this day and has started a new generation)

Grafton
An Imprint of HarperCollins*Publishers*
77–85 Fulham Palace Road,
Hammersmith, London W6 8JB

This expanded edition published by Grafton 1992
9 8 7 6 5 4 3 2 1

First published in Great Britain by
Wildwood House Ltd 1980
under the title *West of Hayle River*

Copyright © Sylvia Priestland 1992

Sylvia Priestland asserts the moral right to
be identified as the author of this work

ISBN 0 586 20987 5

Set in Bembo

Printed in Great Britain by
HarperCollinsManufacturing Glasgow

Contents

Acknowledgements

Ten years ago Sylvia and I published *West of Hayle River*. Through an accident of publishing this went out of print, and we are happy to have the opportunity now to issue it in a revised and expanded form and with the addition of colour to the illustrations. We have also included a chapter on the Isles of Scilly, though purists will remind us that the islands are not properly speaking part of Cornwall. Purists are always tedious companions.

My deepest debt is to the spirits of Robert Hunt, whose *Popular Romances of the West of England* I have used in the Chatto & Windus edition of 1930 and of William Bottrell whose *Hearth-side Stories of West Cornwall* have been invaluably reprinted by Frank Graham of Queen's Terrace, Newcastle upon Tyne. I am also grateful for the publications of the Tor Mark Press of Truro (now Bradford Barton) including S. Daniell's *The Story of Cornwall*, P. Beresford Ellis's *The Story of the Cornish Language*, R.M. Barton's *Cornwall's Scenery and Structure*, D.B. Barton's *The Story of Cornwall's Enginehouses* and *A Guide to the Mines of West Cornwall*, H.V. Williams's *Cornwall's Old Mines* and John Vivian's *Tales of the Cornish Miners*. The Cornwall Archaeological Society's Field Guide No. 2, *The Principal Antiquities of the Land's End District*, is essential, and so are the articles and essays of P. A. S. Pool of Penzance, of which I must cite in particular his pamphlets *The Death of Cornish, The Battle for Penwith, James Stevens – The Diary of a Cornish Farmer* (also in extended book form) and *The Life and Progress of Henry Quick of Zennor*.

No addict of Cornwall can possibly do without the four-volume anthology drawn from the files of the *West Briton* 1810–99 by Rita M. Barton and published 1970–4 by Bradford

Barton. Daphne du Maurier's *Vanishing Cornwall* has also been an inspiration. Of modern guidebooks, John Betjeman's *Shell Guide* (with many photographs by John Piper) and Nikolaus Pevsner's *The Buildings of England – Cornwall* remain standard. I have the church pamphlets of every parish in Penwith, but I owe special thanks to Canon Shane Cotter of Zennor for showing me Robert Morton Nance's material on St Azenor (or, as I like to believe, Senara). Among the older books I have read are Blight's *Week at the Land's End*, Wilkie Collins's *Rambles Beyond Railways*, C.G. Harper's *The Cornish Coast*, Arthur Salmon's *The Cornwall Coast*, A.K. Hamilton Jenkin's *Cornwall and the Cornish* and *Cornish Homes and Customs*, and Thomas's *Ancient and Modern History of Mount's Bay* (1831). Aubrey Burl's encyclopaedic *The Stone Circles of the British Isles* has been invaluable, as have the maps of the Ordnance Survey. I have used the 1975–6 editions of Morton Nance's English–Cornish and Cornish–English dictionaries (The Cornish Language Board). I make my bow to the devoted work of the Old Cornwall Societies, and am grateful to Quentin Bell and Angelica Garnett for permission to use my closing quotation from Virginia Woolf's *Moments of Being* (Sussex University Press, ed. Jeanne Schulkin).

Of the newer books on the Isles of Scilly I am particularly indebted to Ernest Kay's *Isles of Flowers* (1956) and above all to Professor Charles Thomas's *Exploration of a Drowned Landscape* (1985).

From the owner of Trove (all that remains of the old Levelis home) we received much valuable and scholarly information. We must thank her and other owners at Trewoofe, Pendeen Manor, Carn Cobba, Kenegie and Rosemorran for information and for access to take photographs – as indeed we thank all those whose property appears in our pictures. Our general thanks are due to the Jelberts of Carnelloe, our friendly landlords for years, and to the people of Zennor parish as a whole for their tolerance of our presence in their midst. Perhaps I should include the landlords of the Gurnard's Head Hotel, the Tinner's Arms and the Engine Inn and most of the public houses in Penwith, but selection can be invidious.

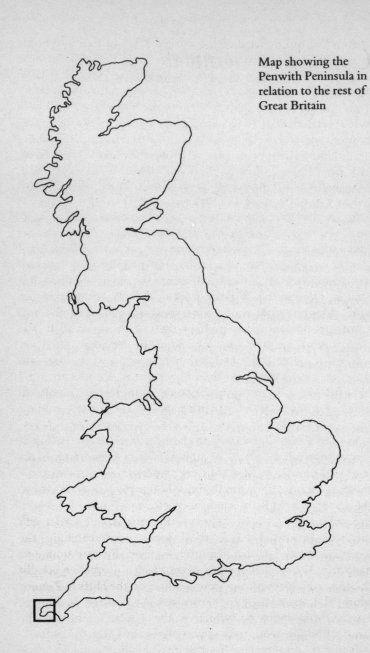

Map showing the
Penwith Peninsula in
relation to the rest of
Great Britain

Cornwall's Cornwall

The man at the Engine Inn said: 'You're not really Cornish unless you're from west of Hayle River.'

Seeing that the Engine Inn is at Cripplescase, about half-way between Splattenridden and Skillywadden and a good four miles west of Hayle, everyone present agreed. Folk from Camborne might just squeeze in, but people from Liskeard and Launceston, Falmouth and Truro, could as well be from Devon. Here in this final toe-joint of Britain, roughly fifteen miles long by five miles wide, was concentrated the real essence of Cornishness, perhaps the last drops of it. It was Cornwall's Cornwall, the very end of the very end. There are softer, more comfortable corners further east before you reach the Tamar, but west of Hayle River we like to think only the fittest have survived, people who greet each other on deserted January mornings with a special nod that means: 'We *know*.'

I say 'we' although I have no claim by birth to citizenship of this extraordinary place. My grandfathers came from Scotland and the Isle of Man, but ever since my parents took me to West Cornwall for the summer holidays, year after year in the 1930s, I have been trying to graft myself onto it. Sylvia, my wife, who grew up believing that the Lake District was the real Promised Land, took some years catching the Cornish fever; but our children – especially our youngest daughter, Diana – fell instant victims to it. In 1970 we bought the lease of a former mine count-house on the cliffs at Zennor (now, alas, exhausted) and now claim the dual nationalities of London and Penwith (which is the official name for the Land's End peninsula, unless you prefer the Latin Bolerium).

It might have been more accurate, if less romantic, to speak of west of the A30 or west of the Great Western Railway rather than west of the Hayle River, for strictly speaking they mark more exactly the frontier behind which I confine myself. If the sea were to rise about fifty feet, as I suppose it might do over the next millennium or two, Penwith would show its independence by becoming an island. Spiritually, it is one already. Because it is the ultimate destination, because you cannot pass through it on the way to anywhere beyond it, Penwith is its own justification. The fortunes of economics have emphasized that. For although there is farming and fishing and the remains of mining (and the peninsula would be a museum without them), these are at the mercy of better placed competitors. It is now only to the visitor – call him a tourist if you must – that Penwith can offer something without substitute, its own presence.

I must try hard to avoid guidebook sentimentality. There are certainly other parts of Britain – not to mention Brittany – where you can find granite coves and moors and even dolmens and menhirs. The point is that Penwith has at least two added dimensions, one physical and the other meta-physical. The physical one is, quite simply, the quality of light. To be in Penwith is to be suspended in light. The air is permanently humid, free of dust and smog, and it transmits the light in startling and dramatic ways. It strikes down from the sky, bounces off the sea and echoes to and fro between the two, shouting as it goes. It is new and fresh and good to breathe – you don't feel that a dozen other people have used it before you – and it conveys a sense of freedom that the artists who have come to St Ives and Newlyn grasp instinctively. The best of them have not attempted to paint Penwith directly: it is almost too picturesque in itself for that. But the clarity of vision, and the freedom, have enabled them to abstract from it, to see the shapes and relationships that really count. Added to which, being exposed to the natural rhythms of the sun and the year and the tides is good for the nerves.

The metaphysical dimension of Penwith, the one which I hope to exploit in my text while Sylvia exploits the other in her photographs, has to do with its unequalled richness in folklore. It is one of the few areas in the British Isles to have preserved – or rather to have had preserved for it – a wide range of legends and superstitions. These tales are very specific as to people and places, so that it is possible to reconstruct them on the spot, to imagine them happening and to guess their true significance. There are elements in them which can be traced far beyond Penwith and back into our Indo-European origins. Elements, too, no doubt, which will delight the Freudian analyst. I suppose that story-tellers everywhere must use the same basic ingredients. But in the far west of Cornwall their stories became thoroughly naturalized, acquiring a distinctively local costume and accent. Thus the tales give meaning to the places and the places to the tales. In Penwith we can come closer not just to history but to tribal pre-history than anywhere else in England.

There are two people to thank for what we know: Robert Hunt, whose activities as a folklore collector ranging from the 1820s through the 1860s were published as *Popular Romances of the West of England*, which has been raided ever since by opportunists like myself; and William Bottrell, a Penwith man by birth, whose newspaper columns in the *Cornish Telegraph* actually supplied Hunt with many of his items. Nevertheless, in his capacity as secretary of the Royal Cornwall Polytechnic Society, Hunt did travel a good deal in the far west, where, as he tells us, he 'elicited the old stories of which the people were beginning to be ashamed'; and we also know he employed a country postman from St Ives to do research for him. Bottrell seems to have relied more on his own leg-work. He had the good fortune to have met, as a boy in St Levan, an old blind soldier called Anthony James. 'Uncle Anthony' was one of the last of the old Cornish Droll-tellers, led from farm to farm by a boy, playing the fiddle and singing his tales in irregular rhyming verse. Bottrell also knew a second Droll-teller in St Just, a man called Billy Frost who 'used to go round to the Feasts in the neighbouring parishes, and be well entertained at the public houses for the sake of his drolls'. Both these wandering minstrels were alive in 1829.

Theirs was a peculiarly Celtic form of entertainment, characteristic of a society that lived scattered about the landscape in small farm settlements, rather than concentrated in villages and towns. It called for intimacy and attention to personal detail, for a strong sense of gossip and knowledge of one's audience. I cannot honestly say that anything like it flourishes in the Land's End peninsula today, though that grand old folk-singer Brenda Wootton still keeps alive the glories of the 1970s in her eyrie up by the Ding Dong mine. If the old tales were being forgotten in Hunt's time, they are totally out of currency now. Only the Victorian collectors and the middle-class preservationists of our own times have prevented their disappearance. The last trace of Droll-telling to linger on was a certain Cornish penchant for writing bad verse. But I do not think even that has survived the Television.

It is normal to describe the Cornish as part of the Celtic Fringe, and they are seated at the conferences of European Celts along with the Bretons, the Welsh, the Manx, Irish and Scots, where two or three Cornishmen will always turn up wearing a saffron kilt of doubtful provenance. But it is easy to see they have more in common with Brittany and Wales (the southern or Brythonic group) than with the northern Goidelic countries. And physically it is obvious that the people of Penwith have a great deal more of the Mediterranean and Iberian in them than they have of the blond beasts from the north.

The Celts were latecomers to Cornwall, perhaps crossing from north-western France around 500 B.C. They brought with them the Iron Age and imposed it on peoples who had been in the peninsula at least two thousand years earlier, through the Stone and Bronze Ages, and who had built most of the granite monuments which give the Land's End area its haunting elderness. It is not too far-fetched to imagine these original occupants of southern England being squeezed westwards, gradually concentrated into Penwith and the Lizard – a backwater that led nowhere – and being left there to preserve the ancient ways.

They were not quite as isolated as that, however. Even in the Bronze Age there was a good deal of sea-going trade, and for centuries the sea was the best link available between

Penwith and the outside world. The peninsula was a convenient staging-post between France, Ireland and Wales, and it had its own exports. Penwith stone axeheads found their way all over England, and Cornish tin and copper went to make the bronze for the Bronze Age. From the rusting cars and derelict farm equipment that litter the fields today, this present must be the Scrap-iron Age.

The Romans subdued Devon and ventured into Cornwall, but found it too uncouth for civilized settlement on a large scale. Already, seaborne invaders, lodged in the folk memory as 'Danes', had set up Gibraltar-like bases on the promontory cliff-castles: Gurnard's Head, Bosigran, Cape Cornwall and the Logan Rock are striking examples, and most of them have nearby beaches for landing boats. There are still at least two natural fortresses known as 'Castel-an-Dinas', supposedly 'Castle of the Danes', and there is an ancient tradition of an unpopular red-headed minority in the region. But whether they really were Danes or a Celtic strain from Brittany or Anglo-Saxons from some more easterly part of the continent, there is no doubt that the people of Cornwall had an even fiercer struggle to preserve their way of life once the Romans had left in the fifth century A.D. Now they were up against the Saxons, who named their land West Wales (the West Foreigners) or Cornu-Wales (the Horn of Foreigners).

Those dark years may well have included the age of the legendary Arthur. You must look further east, to Tintagel and Camelford, to find a place for the Round Table. Dozmary Pool on Bodmin Moor is as promising a place as any I know for an arm to emerge and take back Excalibur. But there are prophecies attributed to Merlin involving Penwith, and a tale of Arthur, aided by nine vassal kings, wiping out a 'Danish' army in a great battle by a mill near the Land's End. A storm blew up that shattered the enemy fleet, and Arthur and his nine kings dined in triumph round the Table Rock at Sennen. It would have been natural enough for the invaders to have landed at Whitesand Bay, just below Sennen, and to have used Maen Castle on the cliffs between there and Land's End. As for the mill, which is said to have 'ground with the blood of Danish warriors', the name given is Vellan-druchar.

The 2½-inch map (only) marks Vellyn–druchia as a ruined cottage about a mile northeast of St Buryan, on a fork of the stream that runs down to Lamorna.

In the end, the Saxon King Athelstan of Wessex conquered even Penwith, and the Celtic Church and its culture were repressed. Little more than a century later it was the turn of the Normans, but like the Romans they seemed to care little for the extreme west. They built no castles in or near Penwith – even St Michael's Mount was originally an abbey rather than a fortress – and although they thoroughly disapproved of the unRomish Celtic saints, they failed to dislodge them from the parishes and almost nothing has survived of their church-building activities in the peninsula. One does not sense a Norman presence here.

Tin-streaming became increasingly important to Cornwall from the thirteenth century onwards, but the main centres of production were in the eastern parts of the county. Nor did Penwith compete with Looe and Falmouth and Fowey as centres of shipping and piracy. The fact is, it was always too remote, too bleak and too poor to attract anyone of sub-stance. There was no local baron, not even enough well-to-do gentry to make a substantial contribution to one of the periodic revolts that marched on Exeter and London out of the West Country. The revolts of 1497 (against taxes) and 1549 (against the English Prayer Book) were largely manned by East Cornishmen; though a century later Penwith under-lined its record as a sanctuary for lost causes by providing the Royalist standard with a refuge on St Michael's Mount. It fell in 1645, and the peninsula was laid waste by famine, plague and Puritan preachers. This was the beginning of the end for the old Cornwall, for with the coming of the eighteenth century the appalling roads began to improve and along them advanced industry, commerce and administration.

You have only to look at a map of Cornwall – compared with one of, say, Kent – to realize that it is literally in a different language. Instead of Sevenoaks and Tonbridge, Dartford and Longfield, you are enveloped in incantations like Rose-an-Grouse, Crows-an-wra, Trythogga, Noon-gallas, Mulfra, Boswednack and Woon Gumpus. Such relics of the Cornish language as are left to us today give the impression of a rough, workaday peasant tongue that was good enough for farming, fishing and pre-industrial mining but never developed any literature to compare with Welsh or Irish. This is not entirely fair. After the defeat of the Celtic Church in A.D. 664 and Athelstan's conquest in the tenth century, many of the ancient manuscripts must have been destroyed and the people were obliged to accept Latin as their main language of worship. We do know, however, that a number of religious formulas, including the Ten Command-ments, the Lord's Prayer and the Apostles' Creed were recited in Cornish and were still known in Penwith as late as 1600. However, most people by then were bilingual in Cornish and English (or 'naughty Englysshe' as one disapproving visitor put it), and more and more people east of Hayle River were using English only. Even then, these anglicized Cornish were regarded as a barbarous tribe: 'Their ale is stark nought as pigges had wrastled therein.'

The Cornish language might have been saved, like Welsh, if Parliament had given both languages equal treatment. By the Act of 1563, Wales got its own translations of the Bible and Prayer Book; but Cornwall was accounted too small to bother about. Moreover, the Cornish had recently shown themselves far too sympathetic to the ways of Rome. And so, with the outside world pressing in from the east once more, the last hope of establishing a permanent reservoir and standard of the language in the Church was lost. By the latter half of the seventeenth century visitors were reporting that although the old folk in the Land's End and Lizard areas still used it, the days of Cornish were clearly numbered.

There was, perhaps, one last hope. There seems to have been a flowering of religious drama in Cornwall from about 1450 up to the Reformation. Plays lasting up to three days in length were staged in arenas such as can still be seen at St Just, with the object of teaching the Bible to a people who – even if they were literate – could find no scripture in their own language. This drama, if it had been allowed to develop, might have saved Cornish. But nobody bothered to print it, the Bible arrived in English, and the surviving plays were put down as sinfully Romish. Few manuscripts have reached us today.

In the nick of time, from the middle of the seventeenth century, a handful of part-time scholars began collecting Cornish words and phrases. One of them noted, 'We find the young speak it less and less and worse and worse, and so it is like to decay.' The religious split with the continent and enmity between England and France had meant cutting the long-surviving links with Brittany, originally colonized by the Cornish. Furthermore, increasing numbers of outsiders were settling in Cornwall, especially in ports like Falmouth. It was not smart or commercial to speak Cornish.

By the middle of the eighteenth century the great anti-quarian Dr William Borlase of Ludgvan was persuaded that the language was already extinct. In this he was certainly wrong, for in the 1770s at least four native Cornish-speakers were discovered, among them that celebrated curmudgeon Dolly Pentreath of Mousehole, who was alleged to have been the last of all when she died at the age of 102. Neither of those claims was true, either. Most authorities accept the year 1800 as the point beyond which there was nobody living who could use Cornish fluently in daily speech; but even that will not do for the parish of Zennor, whose church wall bears a plaque in memory of John Davey of Boswednack, who died in 1891 and was claimed as the last person to have been brought up with any considerable traditional knowledge of the Cornish tongue. Today, thanks mainly to the labours of the late Robert Morton Nance (1873–1959), whose dark green 'First Steps in Cornish' I used to study at school when I was supposed to have been studying Greek, Cornwall is peppered with revivalists who can probably speak better Cornish than Dolly Pentreath ever did. Still, a good deal of it is borrowed from Breton, Welsh or Middle English, and to me the whole operation seems rather like putting a corpse on a heart-lung machine and claiming it is alive.

> *An lavar coth yu lavar gwyr:*
> *Byth dorn re ver, th'an davas re hyr.*
> *Mez den heb davas a-gollas y-dir.*

Or that's as well as I can remember my Morton Nance at some forty years' remove. If I have got it anywhere near right, it should mean: 'The old saying is a true one: Long on talk means short on action. But the man who lost his tongue, lost his land.' And maybe that is what is happening to Cornwall's Cornwall.

But even if they are not all native born or Cornish-speakers, there are still plenty of people in Penwith ready to defend it against those whom they regard as being the wrong sort of settlers. Think of the words 'environment' or 'ecology' or even 'planning permission' and you will begin picking up the mood. There is no question that the Land's End peninsula is (in the official term) an Area of Outstanding Natural Beauty. The National Trust has been gratefully collecting chunks of clifftop all the way round. But natural beauty does not pay the rent or feed the children, and local farmers are under constant temptation to sell off or develop bits of it for more lucrative purposes. You can't sit in front of the view with a collecting box: the tourists won't pay unless you have somewhere for them to stay, and when you do provide it they all want to come in August.

There is the story of the Englishman, the Irishman, the Scotsman, the Welshman and the Cornishman who were shot up together on to the Moon. When they arrived, the Englishman and the Irishman started a fight, the Scot opened a distillery, the Welshman a chapel – while the Cornishman hung out a Bed and Breakfast sign. Come the holiday season, and the walls of Penwith blossom with little banners proclaiming 'B & B'. Even when (for tax reasons) no attention is drawn to it, you can be fairly sure that the owners of every other cottage and farm are sleeping in a caravan at the back, while their bedrooms are packed with tourists, some-times referred to as 'emmets' (ants) or 'BSVs' (Bloody Summer Visitors).

For the native Penwithian, the holiday trade is one long struggle to turn admiration into hard cash. It is debatable whether the alternatives are any more desirable. Over the past twenty years, there has been a series of battles over the Land's End landscape, either to install caravan parks and holiday chalets or else to open up mines and quarries – or worse. The painter Patrick Heron, who lives in the aptly named Eagle's Nest, a superb Victorian house between St Ives and St Just, unmasked a plot by the Ministry of Defence to turn the coastal strip there into a commando assault ground, with waves of helicopters descending rowdily onto the moors. A later discovery of his, aided by the *Guardian* newspaper, was a scheme to sell off parcels of the Lady Downs, overlooking Zennor. In 1960 the whole parish was literally up in arms over the plans of a big international mining group to reopen the defunct Carnelloe mine, and some of the inhabitants still aren't speaking to each other because of it. A little later, someone wanted to start open-cast mining on the old Ding Dong mine site, in the very middle of the peninsula; and although that, and a further scheme for china clay working, were defeated, the enormous excavations of the Amalgamated Roadstone Company outside Gulval continue unabated. *And* there was the converted piggeries scandal at Towednack, *and* the project for chalets at the Gurnard's Head, not to mention an unplanned riding school and the sneaking in of sundry campsites and caravans where it is hoped they will not be noticed.

You don't have to drive far into Penwith before you begin to spot the abandoned barns and Methodist chapels. The faith has dwindled, and farming nowadays uses one or two big centralized hangars. The cast-offs look just the thing for converting into holiday or retirement cottages, and many a farmer has had the dream of turning them into hard cash. A ruined shell on a moor could easily fetch fifteen thousand pounds with a bit of land round it, or an unused wing of the farmyard turn into lettable self-catering units.

But is it socially desirable, is it good planning? Local officials have sometimes declared they would rather see a barn fall down than become a house. They have had an understandable dread of populating Penwith either with retired folk demanding health services, young marrieds demanding schools for their children, or anybody adding extra traffic to the narrow lanes.

Penwithians, too, have been heard to grumble about

'foreigners' bidding over the heads of the locals and robbing young Cornish couples of their ancestral cottages. Mebyon Curnow, the Sons of Cornwall Party, got their biggest vote (1,662) in the St Ives constituency in 1979. But there is a fair argument to be put on the other side, that the native Penwithian shows a strong liking for a nice new council-house near one of the towns, leaving the foreigners to rescue and restore the damp and isolated granite cottage.

The price of natural beauty is eternal vigilance. But if one is tempted to chide the Penwithian for not caring much whether some holy well or haunted carn is bulldozed away for a bungalow or a broiler unit, and for leaving the environmental battle to middle-class campaigners, it is just as well to remember once more that the native has a living to make, not just a holiday to take. His ancestors helped to form the landscape in the past and (although I should not care to gamble on this happening again) it was yesterday's industrial sacrilege that became today's picturesque ruin.

Penwithians are friendly and courteous towards their visitors; they are 'well brought up' in an old-fashioned way. But it cannot be easy having strangers treating your homeland as a picnic ground; and there must always be a certain tension between those who want to treat the peninsula as a work of art, a land of legend, and those who have to make their living out of its very soil. Some of the pain and hardship of that living seems to have soaked into the landscape, giving a hard backbone to its picturesqueness.

Touring the Horizon

Before I try to penetrate below the surface of this landscape, I should like to give the reader a frame within which to work. Penwith consists essentially of a granite dome with slatey killas and tough greenstone at intervals along the northern coast. This, being exposed to the full force of the incoming Atlantic, shows a fiercer, harsher cliffscape than Land's End and the south coast, where the granite has been worn into architectural blocks and stacks. Up on the moors, which peak at less than eight hundred feet, you will find cheesewrings and citadels of weathered moorstone.

Though this does not pretend to be a comprehensive guidebook, I hope it will persuade many readers to explore Penwith on the spot. I still assume that most will go by car (though the rail journey has its special magic) and that most readers will be prepared to park-and-walk a good deal. In getting to Cornwall you have your choice of the M4–M5 route to Exeter or the M3–A303–A30; but, either way, I recommend the A38 on to Saltash, rather than sparring with the caravans and lorries all the way via Okehampton. In desperate circumstances there are long, rustic alternatives involving South Molton, Great Torrington and Holsworthy. But I assume we begin this tour at Hayle.

I admire hikers and bikers and they are certainly more ecological than motorists. Best of all, in many ways, would be the horse. But a car is good to have in Penwith for several reasons: the buses are inadequate, the weather can be soaking, riding and walking are no fun at all when the holiday traffic is running and, in spite of the lack of space, there seems to be no such thing in Penwith as a straight line. The distances are always longer than you expected. Fortunately, you cannot possibly reach all your objectives by car. There are plenty of paths and tracks where wheels cannot go and where foot is the only way.

What I propose to do now is to drive you, in imagination, round the edge of the peninsula, giving you a general idea of it and, incidentally, disposing of the four or five towns which will not concern us much again. For towns, interesting though they may be, are not Celtic or pre-Celtic entities, they have not absorbed the genius of the place, and they play very little part in the folk-history and legends we are going to rediscover.

A map is essential if this is anything more than an armchair ride for you. The most convenient basic sheet is the Ordnance Survey 1:50,000 series, Sheet 203, entitled Land's End and The Lizard. If you are bitten deeply with the Penwith bug, you may want the 2½-inch series (for example, sheets SW43 and SW44 cover an important area from Zennor on the north coast to Penberth on the south) or the newer green-covered 1:25,000 series. But in both cases you will need two or more sheets, and the places you want always seem to be on the overlaps.

A word about motoring, before we set off. Even if you are blind to landscape, this is no place for speeding. If I had my way the entire peninsula would be under a thirty-miles-an-hour limit. There are few stretches even on the A30 or A3071 where as much as forty is justifiable. Penwith's lanes are narrow and banked high on either side with stone walls, known here as 'hedges', so that it is very hard to know what is coming. The horn, of course, is no substitute for concentration and good brakes; but it seems to me that no-one in Penwith should be ashamed of hooting. This does not apply to hooting at herds of cows, encountered on their way to milking. The only thing to do in that case is to lie back and enjoy them. I almost included the monster coaches which fancy the scenic route to Land's End along the north coast, but nobody could possibly enjoy meeting them. As they seem to travel in convoys one can only counsel patience, or making the visit outside the holiday season – say May or October. And beware of the increasing numbers of Belgian, French and

German cars whose drivers cannot see quickly round the bends because their steering-wheels are on the wrong side.

Let us begin in Hayle, at Foundry Square under the Great Western Railway viaduct, once the hub of this by no means negligible (but now rather battered) town, still the gathering of some useful shops and tradesmen, such as a dentist. The shops include a typically Cornish bakery and a collection of boutiques under the roof of a disused Methodist chapel which would have converted more appropriately into an opera house. In the past few years Hayle has been bypassed by the A30 which does not strictly go there any more, but soars across country in the direction of St Erth. But the end of the world forecast by Hayle's shopkeepers has not come to pass and the town is, on the whole, better for it and not visibly the poorer. One lamentable loss which cannot be connected with the bypass is the Naval Surplus Stores – a treasure house of ancient tools and uniforms and catering equipment – which used to occupy yet another abandoned chapel just back of the war-memorial. It dressed a whole generation of my children in Luftwaffe tunics and Dartmoor jackets.

Whether Hayle will be made any richer by the plans of that playboy of the western world, Mr Peter de Savary, is still a matter of waiting and seeing. We have been promised dredging and quayside apartments and a marina and three hundred houses, all of which one could well imagine, for Hayle today is full of gaps which a builder could fill. Whether it will really overcome the planning process is one thing, and whether it will add a single bed to the housing stock of the local people another; for the yuppification of Penwith seems bound to follow the boats. Nevertheless, I must confess I should like to see a little daring in Hayle, even at the expense of some vulgarity.

It is the usual thing to groan about Hayle. One Edwardian guidebook refers to it as 'an exceedingly ill-favoured place with no redeeming features' but that is not true. Get off the main road and it is full of redeeming features: a Cornish pasty factory full of jolly women folding and crimping the Cornishman's one true luncheon, a Romano-British tomb complete with inscription, and just off the B3302 the pleasant homes of Millpond Avenue, which overlook a couple of large ponds crowded with ducks and seagulls.

Few people realize that Hayle was one of the great engineering centres of the industrial revolution. The basic reason was that Cornish mines were wet and needed constant pumping, first by horse-pumps, then by Newcomen engines, then by Richard Trevithick's. Hayle was an ideal place to cast the engines and pumps because coal could be brought in by sea from Wales: it was already brought in to smelt copper in the Hayle suburb of Copperhouse. So it was at Hayle that Harvey's made their gigantic single-cylinder engines with diameters of one hundred inches and more. They lasted for ever and went all over the world, and Hayle shipped them as well as made them – or did until Harvey's and the rival firm at Copperhouse quarrelled over who was responsible for keeping the estuary clear, and the port silted up. Nor was this the only quarrel between the two. It is perfectly obvious to anyone who keeps his eyes open that in Penwith – being so far to the west of Greenwich – it stays light later than it does in London; and well past the middle of the last century it was common to observe Cornish Time, which was twenty minutes behind the capital. The Copperhouse firm kept their clock accordingly, but when the railway arrived Harvey's confused the populace by setting theirs in agreement with London.

The port of Hayle did not deal only in engines. In the 1840s it shipped cast-iron components to Bristol for the Clifton suspension bridge and pieces to London for the bridge at Hungerford. Steamers plied to Cardiff and Cork, as well as Bristol, though emigrants for the New World had to seek bigger ships elsewhere. Today what is left of the port is sadly depressed, as is employment generally in Penwith. The last I heard, unemployment had doubled in four years and reached a percentage more than three times the national average. The coal-burning power station at the mouth of the estuary was finally closed down, and even the piles of old iron that earned Hayle the unofficial title of Scrap Metal Capital of Cornwall were being cleared away and the quay stood empty.

You leave the town by the A30, past the Romano-British

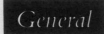

General

North is at the top of the page on all maps.

The maps 1–5 are sketch maps only, based on personal observation. They will help you to locate the walks in the book and pick out salient features on them, many of which cannot be found on other maps, but they are not accurate as to scale or topography.

If you are proposing to follow the walks we strongly urge you to equip yourself with Ordnance Survey maps – either 1:25000 or 1:50000 scale. They include contours, which our maps, since they are not the product of surveys, obviously cannot show.

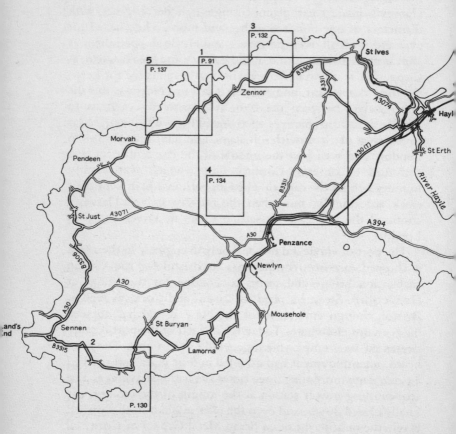

tumulus, along the estuary of Hayle River. Usually the tide is out and bird-watchers can stop to enjoy the waders. This is the only time the river gives any impression of being a wide Missouri. Mostly it is no more than a rustic stream that starts in a pond near Praze-an-Beeble, turns north at Relubbus (where there is a Moskvitch car dealer) and slides through the cow-pastures towards St Erth, where it contrives to hurry a bit as it passes under the mediaeval bridge. They say that ships used to get that far up from the sea, though today you would be hard put to it to reach the place with a punt. Nevertheless, St Erth is not to be sniffed at. There is a good pub in the centre of the village, and the church – well, it might have suffered worse at the hands of its Puritan desecrators and its eighteenth- and nineteenth-century restorers. Just inside the churchyard gate there is a stone announcing that 'Within this enclosure lie enterred the bodies of Six Persons who in the year 1832 died of the awful visitation of Cholera'. Cholera was the scourge of Cornwall for some forty years from that date. But it still seems sad that St Erth laid its victims to rest without names to them.

If you visit St Erth you have to come off the A30 at the signpost pointing to it. Returning to the main road, my tour continues along the estuary and then forks right towards St Ives – which we won't visit yet. Instead, after going under a small bridge and then right at a mini-roundabout, we take a very pleasant first-on-the-left towards Land's End and Zennor, the first real relaxation after too much A30. It takes you through woods and shrubbery, past turnings to Trencrom and Cripplesease and Carbis Bay onto the B3311 – the Penzance to St Ives road – where you turn right, pass by Halsetown (another good pub), the St Ives Reservoir and arrive at the extraordinary B3306.

By myself, I would answer the call of the west and turn instantly left. Wild donkeys will not drag me into St Ives in the summer, and if you do go (as you certainly should) you should turn right down the hill and find parking half-way down – then walk. It is not fair to you or St Ives to attempt to drive through it. One other good reason for taking this route is that at the top of the hill on the left stands the pottery of the late, great master Bernard Leach. Craft pottery is not really native to Penwith: Leach started it all and taught most of those who are any good. It remains to be seen how things will go now his influence is waning; I suspect there is already less potting in Penwith and more hand-weaving and knitting. But pottering among the wayside potteries can still be a rewarding experience, and the bins of 'seconds' at the Leach Pottery itself are extremely good value. (My oriental cats eat, as befits their origins, off Leach seconds.)

St Ives once did reasonably well out of tin. But the real purpose of its being was fish: in the mid-nineteenth century it was probably the busiest fishing port in the world, with 250 seine (or sean) nets scooping up pilchards by the million and exporting them, pressed and salted, to the Mediterranean countries. Said the old toast:

> Here's a health to the Pope, may he live to repent
> And add six more months to the term of his Lent;
> And tell all his vassals from Rome to the Poles,
> There's nothing like pilchards for saving their souls.

Alas, the pilchards scarcely outlasted the nineteenth century and the same was true of the tin. But before that happened a small trickle of artists, inspired by the open-air activities of their French colleagues and given greater freedom to roam by the railways, discovered St Ives on the north coast and Newlyn on the south. A certain rivalry still continues between the Newlyn Orion Gallery and the Penwith Gallery in St Ives; for although the Penwith traditionally can claim the great names – the Hepworths and the Herons – it cannot be denied that from the 1970s the Newlyn had the outreach and publicity, thanks to the flair of its curator John Halkes. It does not matter a great deal to the public, for the two towns are now so close together by car, and there is in effect a unified West Penwith community of artists which you can view in both places. But who knows, the balance may be swinging back to St Ives: the spring of 1990 brought the announcement that not only was the Tate Gallery prepared to lodge its collection of Cornish paintings in St Ives, but something like two million pounds was to be spent on building a gallery for them on the splendid site of the old gas works, overlooking the beach at Porthmeor; and thanks to a combination of local government, European Community and foundation finance, the money was largely assured.

With the Penwith Gallery and the St Ives Society of Artists (which maintains a steady output of red sails in the sunset and daffodils in the springtime, which it markets in a handsome disused chapel, down by the harbour) plus small commercial galleries like the Wills' Lane and the Salt House, St Ives is becoming an interesting market-place in its own right. It is also more of a living-place for artists than Newlyn, which is rather too much into the business of fish these days. If you want to meet real live artists, and buy their work at realistic prices, St Ives is the place. Artists like Roy Ray, Bob Devereux, Roy Walker will take time off to explain why they are doing what they do. (They do not do red sails in the sunset, by the way.)

Picturesqueness is the blessing and curse of St Ives. In addition to turning out thousands of canvases that say no more than anyone can see, it draws in thousands of holiday-makers to walk around seeing it. It provides them with boarding houses, ice-creams, fish and chips, beer, disco-theques, early editions of the *Sun*, gulls to feed, snaps to take, souvenirs to buy and a great deal of high-grade sand to lie on. You can surf at the beach called Porthmeor, which is Euro-approved.

And hidden away behind all this, revelling in the light and the studios and ignoring the visitors, are – or have been – some of the most distinguished names of modern English painting and sculpture: names like Ben Nicholson, Peter Lanyon, Patrick Heron, Alfred Wallis, Naum Gabo and – biggest of all, I suppose – Barbara Hepworth who, in her own words 'gradually discovered the remarkable, pagan landscape which lies between St Ives, Penzance and Land's End'.

Barbara Hepworth's Trewyn Studio, and its garden full of her sculpture, are in a back street not far from the parish church and open to the public. The fire in which she died damaged the building very little and her workshops are still as she left them – even down to the note on a row of files 'Please do not move the tools from this bench – B.H.'. The garden, with its bamboos and heckling seagulls, contains more than a dozen of her favourite pieces, including two really striking late works – *Fallen Images* and *Conversation with Magic Stones* – which are clearly inspired by the ritual stone circles of Penwith. This garden, and the little Celtic-style chapel on the promontory known as the Island, are the best things about St Ives.

But perhaps I am unfair to it, for it is brilliantly conserved. Visit St Ives off-season and you can admire it for the same reasons as Virginia Woolf, who praised its utter lack of period and called it 'a windy, noisy, fishy, vociferous, narrow-streeted town; the colour of a mussel or a limpet; like a bunch of rough shell-fish, oysters or mussels, all crowded together'.

She might also have mentioned – for it was going strong in her day – the enchanting little railway that shuttles between St Ives and St Erth, defying all temptations, however obvious, to close it for economy reasons and substitute a bus. The railway serves Carbis Bay, just round the corner from St Ives, and just round the corner from the Edwardian age, too, for Carbis Bay has not changed since the 1920s except that the boarding houses have changed into self-catering flats with sea views. If you have what I understand is known as a 'toddler' it is absolutely ideal. The sand is like soft sugar.

So back up out of St Ives and along the B3306 towards St Just and Land's End – and watch out for dangerous corners all the way. The road here follows the line of demarcation between the bottom of the moors and the top of the farmable coastal strip, with the sea to the right of you, peacock green or slate blue or mullet grey. There are actually two other routes between you and the sea, the coastal path (which is hard going and calls for gumboots), and the ancient, stiled footway linking the farmsteads and along which, they say, the coffins were carried to the churchyard.

This is a breathtaking road, but I must warn you that there are few places where you can pull off it. It runs through what used to be called 'The High Countries', the wild parishes of Towednack, Zennor and Morvah, and it still gives me a high-altitude feeling as if I were in Tibet, with the clear light zinging past my ears and the wind dazzling my eyes. It is a treeless country, so, with nothing to limit the horizon, the dome of the sky overhead seems bigger than it does in counties that are actually more spacious.

At the highest point in the road, to the right, stands the Eagle's Nest with the old Parish Poorhouse of Zennor beside it, and far below, the cottages of Tregerthen where D.H. Lawrence and Katherine Mansfield tried to settle during the First World War. Katherine's partner, John Middleton Murry, could not abide the seagulls (a special plague to some upcountry people) and the Cornish suspected the Lawrences of being German spies and hounded them out of Penwith. One allegation was that they had been signalling with oil lamps to German submarines; but the local tradition now admits that Lawrence used to read in bed with the window open and the curtains flapping. If it is any consolation to his ghost, I was once chivvied out of the Gurnard's Head Inn myself as a 'no-good layabout writer'. But that, I hasten to add, was not under the present management.

The Gurnard's Head is approaching, but you cannot see it from the road. First, there is Zennor with its pub, the Tinner's Arms, and its church of which I shall have more to say later. Zennor people were once known as 'Zennor Goats' – whether because they kept them or behaved like them, I do not know. The scarcity of grazing did win the parish the description of being 'where the cow ate the bell-rope', but cows do very well there now. I am not sure that Zennor has kept two other reputations it once had, for being hard-drinking and lusty-singing, but it is still true – as once was written of it – that 'in Zennor, everybody is equal'. It has no use for social class. The parish still celebrates its week-long 'Feast' in mid-May, and it is a great social faux-pas to miss a wedding or a funeral. Zennor people sometimes play elaborate practical jokes on one another, but they respect a network of family loyalties and rally round to lend a hand in time of trouble. They are as tough as granite and almost as long-lived, and they preserve the old way of helping out on each other's farms rather than hire labour from outside.

They also possess a better-than-average pride in their vanishing Cornish heritage. In the churchtown – that is, the village: for to speak of something being 'in Zennor' could mean anywhere in the parish – there is an old mill housing a fascinating museum of bygone implements of the mines and farmsteads. And thanks to the efforts of a notable preservationist, Mr Peter Pool, Zennor has also salvaged the writings of some of its folk authors. I spoke earlier of a capacity for writing bad verse. Perhaps naive or primitive would have been more graceful adjectives. You can see the quality even in the church, which houses a tombstone with the splendidly gloomy inscription:

> Hope, fear, false joy and trouble,
> Are those four winds which daily toss this buble,
> His breath's a vapour and his life's a span,
> Tis glorious misery to be born a man.

But the authors whom Mr Pool has rescued are far from anonymous. You may take your choice between Henry Quick (1792–1857):

> Be pleas'd to buy my little book,
> And don't despise nor overlook;
> Please to take pity on poor Henny,
> I love to earn an honest penny.

Or you may prefer James Stevens (1847–1918):

> I love the Church, I love her ways,
> I love her songs, I love her lays,
> I love her rules, I love her guides,
> I'll stick to her whate'er betides.

Stevens, in fact, is much more significant as a diarist than as a poet. His diaries, kept between 1877 and 1912, are rich with laconic entries like: 'Pulled Grandma's furze 200 faggots and pooked some turfs.' In those days, folk still got their fuel off the moors in the shape either of gorse bundles (faggots of furze) or chunks of peat. I do not know anyone who uses either today. It is the custom, rather, to burn the gorse where it stands so as to let the grass through for grazing.

The coast road curves and swerves onwards past the Gurnard's Head to the long flanks of Carn Galver, where there is a splendid view of the sea from 450 feet up. Here you pass the rock-climbing centre at Bosigran, with its ruined engine-houses by the roadside, and – please – concentrate intensely for the narrow bends at a little hamlet called Rosemergy; no place to take at speed. Indeed the next few miles call for the driver's undivided attention: there is one S-bend hamlet after another.

In the midst of them is Morvah – Miserable Morvah, I am inclined to call it. It certainly isn't what it was in the days of tin, when people rode eagerly 'three on one horse to Morvah Fair'. It was the despair of John Wesley, who doggedly kept coming back to it but found too little conviction of sin and too much backsliding; and in 1813 a pregnant girl who had killed herself was buried at night at Morvah crossroads. The modest church is the only one in Britain dedicated to St Briget of Sweden, and the Swedes have presented it with a flag and some elegant glassware. But I still find it a depressing place and hurry by.

The next tower you see ahead is Pendeen, a mid-Victorian do-it-yourself church, designed by the vicar and built by his parishioners. Pendeen, like its herald Boscaswell, is essentially a mining village, and the last working mine left in the peninsula – Geevor – is at the heart of it. Geevor prospered and survived to the 1980s, thanks to producing a variety of minerals; but the 1990s at last saw the end of its life and there are now only a few maintenance men left below ground. You can visit its museum near the road. Otherwise Pendeen boasts an excellent baker, an all-purpose shop, and a pub called The Radjel (literally, a loose heap of rocks) which until recently was the last of the old Cornish beer houses that I knew, with benches and long scrubbed tables and customers who had been there, like the landlord, for the past fifty years and more. Now there are coloured umbrellas on the terrace.

Beyond Pendeen and more tricky S-bends you pass a

turning on the right down to Botallack, the Pompeii or Luxor of the mining industry – a whole dead city of chimneys and engine-houses and processing floors, with the ruins marching down the cliff to the very water's edge. It was not far from here, at Wheal Owles on 10 January 1893, that the sea burst into the workings and twenty men were drowned. They still lie there, five hundred feet down.

Back to the main road, then, and on to St Just, the last town of any size in England, and here again I must restrain myself from being unkind. I certainly would not be as uncharitable as my Edwardian predecessor, the one who did not care for Hayle. St Just, he said, was 'a dreary town that has seen better days, smug, commonplace . . . without a trace of beauty or interest. Every building is a plain, matter-of-fact square or oblong box with a lid, and they all face arid, expressionless streets . . . Imagine the dullest, smallest provincial town of your acquaintance and further imagine it to be the afternoon of an early-closing day . . ..' St Just is no St Ives, but it is not that bad. Of its pubs the Star Inn is to be preferred (I am not, incidentally, suggesting you should drink your way round this circuit); it has some useful shops which can save you fighting the crowds in Penzance, and it deserves some credit for surviving at all when there is so little mining left. Of its antiquities, the church is well worth entering and on the opposite side of the square is the circular Plan-an-Guare where three-day Miracle Plays were done, wrestling matches held, or revival meetings. Wesley approved of St Just: 'where there is still the largest Society in Cornwall (*he wrote*) and so great a proportion of believers I have not found in all the nation beside'. Well, godliness and dullness do sometimes go together, though perhaps St Just is not the perfect example. Some years ago the vicar abandoned his family and ran off with a *femme fatale* from up-country, and there was talk of witchcraft in the local inns.

There is a tricky manoeuvre as you leave St Just, for you have to turn right for Land's End, still following the B3306, and not charge ahead along what has become the A road to Penzance. This will take you by St Just Aerodrome, a grass field from where you can hire sightseeing flights, and small fixed-wing planes run an alternative to the helicopter service that goes from Penzance. Soon after that you merge into the A30, which rolls you relentlessly through Sennen church-town to the Land's End itself. As you enter Sennen there is a turning to the right that brings you down to Sennen Cove and Whitesand Bay, the most easily got-at beach in Penwith and well-loved by surfers. It was also well-loved by mon-archs or would-be monarchs looking for the first possible place to come ashore: Athelstan c. 930, Stephen in 1135, John in 1210 and the disastrous Perkin Warbeck in 1497 must all have been glad to set foot there. So, in later years, have been a host of fishermen, artists and holidaymakers, as well as the sailors rescued by the last lifeboat in England. A columnist in the *West Briton* in 1899 reported with relief that Sennen Cove had 'no niggers, no char-a-bancs and, greatest blessing of all, no marine band of exiled Germans'. And the Sennen land-lady, he added, though a wretched cook, was scrupulously clean. So, by the way, is the beach which is Euro-approved.

Back on the last mile of the A30 you could hardly miss the way to Land's End if you wanted to, which you might on a crowded day. As the first and last hotel in England comes in sight, marked by the first and last convenience, first and last souvenir shop, first and last pillar box, refuse bin and seagull, there is little option but to park in the first and last car park and head for the first and last hotel – the State House – where the ingenious Mr de Savary has founded another colony. The National Trust wanted Land's End as the crowning jewel in its coastal crown; but money told in the end, and money is expected to justify the investment from now on. I have to say that I personally do not think this is the disaster some of my friends do. To begin with, Mr de Savary's fun park might well be a lot worse and if I were a child who had been dragged to the edge of the known world to look at some sea and some rocks, I should probably be grateful for it. Land's End is not itself breathtakingly beautiful, and by building a tourist attraction there the mob will be kept away from the places nearby that are. Anyway, before you is the Longships Lighthouse, wearing a helicopter on its head, and to your right Cape Cornwall which may appear to be further to the west but is not. Apart from the distant Isles of Scilly, England stops here among the tableaux of shipwrecks and smuggling that Mr de Savary has provided.

Although Land's End is a good deal less spectacular than much of the cliff scenery to the south and east of it, its very finality usually has a sobering effect on people. Once the improved roads and railways began to open up the west, almost everybody who was anybody had to come and have a look. George Fox, the Quaker, rode here in his leather britches and was shocked to find the Land's Enders exploiting the many 'shipwracks' (which they accounted to God's Grace) to their own advantages 'not caring to save the people's lives'. John Wesley pronounced: 'It was an awful sight. But how will these rocks melt away when God ariseth to judgement!' Queen Victoria (accompanied by the Prince Consort and Bertie, Duke of Cornwall) inspected Land's End from the royal yacht and found it 'very fine and rocky'. The Cornish she considered 'a very noisy and talkative race and speak a kind of English hardly to be understood'.

Literary men seem to prefer the Highlands or the Lake District. Tennyson came to Land's End twice and was pestered by celebrity-watchers. The novelist Wilkie Collins (who agreed with me about the misery of Morvah) described Land's End as being sublime beyond description. He and his companion excited the attention of the Land's Enders by walking there with knapsacks on their backs, it being assumed that they must be pedlars with something to sell. Collins heard one tin miner ask another what their wares might be and receive the confident answer 'guinea-pigs'. Any guinea-pig that ventured out of its pack there today would soon get trodden flat.

If you follow the coastal path from Land's End eastward you can now enjoy some of the finest cliff views in Cornwall. But in the car you drive back inland a little and then fork right along the B3315, by places with names like Skewjack and Polgigga, turnings for Porthgwarra, Porthcurno and St Levan, and then for Treen and the Logan Rock. There is a first-rate pub here – Treen is altogether a first-rate place, where farming and sightseeing manage to coexist without either one spoiling the other. But to press on, you plunge down into the Penberth Valley, crawl steeply up the opposite side and reach the top to find the church tower of St Buryan watching you.

It watches you all over this particular arable plateau, for we have long since left northern hills and moorlands and set our course along the lush southern sector of the peninsula, with its deep stream-valleys running down to the sea. If I were a general, I would say that St Buryan commands a strategic road junction in the midst of this sector.

It is typical of Penwith that we have very little idea who the original Buryan or Beriona was. Possibly she was Bruniec, the daughter of an Irish king, possibly she was acquainted with St Patrick and St Piran, just possibly she established her cell at this place in the middle of the fifth century in the midst of a pagan stone circle. It probably developed into a small Celtic monastery, because when Athelstan founded a Saxon church there in 932, as thanksgiving for his conquest of the Scillies, he endowed it to provide a living for a dean and three prebendaries. What is more, he declared it to be immune from secular taxation and treated it, as did his successors for centuries after, as an acceptable gift for royal favourites, most of whom did not trouble to take up residence.

This led to complaints from the Bishops of Exeter, who objected both to the loss of revenue and the lack of discipline at St Buryan. In 1324 King Edward II and Bishop Grandisson made conflicting appointments, the Bishop's man tried to seize the treasury, and there was a fight in the churchyard which the King's man won at the cost of bloodshed. The Bishop was too scared to set foot in the parish, which he described as 'not only the ends of the earth, but the very end of the end thereof', but he did venture as far as St Michael's Mount, where he solemnly pronounced excommunication against those parishioners who had participated in the affray.

It must have been a terrifying moment, with the monks snuffing out and casting down their candles, intoning 'so may their souls be extinguished and handed over to the Devil and his angels for punishment without end in everlasting fire'. Within weeks the brawlers were petitioning for absolution, and the Bishop was able at last to enter St Buryan and preach on the text 'All ye like sheep have gone astray'. Penitence did not last, however. In 1351 the Court ruled that by reason of its tax exemption the parish was a Royal Peculiar and no business of the Bishop's. It was not until 1850 – five hundred years later – that St Buryan was restored to episcopal discipline and its outlying churches of St Levan and St Sennen were established as distinct entities with their own resident vicars. As late as 1814, the Dean of St Buryan was a Londoner who enjoyed a stipend of £800 (a tidy fortune in those days) in return for setting foot in the place once. He was an old soldier who had been ordained by an Irish bishop for the express purpose of enjoying the benefice, and I suspect that the long line of pastoral neglect which he terminated accounts for the history of witchcraft and diabolism which came to be associated with the area – and still is. Over the centuries St Buryan has probably earned the title of the wickedest parish in England: but I have written a small pamphlet on the subject which you can purchase in the church for the good of the fabric.

In the middle of Buryan churchtown my route now bids you turn right, opposite the church, and take the lane that leads towards the sea and rejoins the B3315. You turn left at this junction, beside a stubby Celtic cross (the roads round St Buryan have them every few hundred yards – perhaps as protection against the diabolism). Very soon you will pass through a positive open-air museum of antiquities: on the right, two more crosses, a topless tomb and the celebrated Merry Maidens stone circle; on the left, various stones marking the battlefield of Boleit where Athelstan finally crushed the mainland Cornish.

A Z-bend later you descend the hillside into the Lamorna Valley. By all means take the turning at the bottom that leads to the cove. I should park at the pub and spend a few minutes following the lane that leads round the back of it to an extremely pretty mill; then back to the pub and walk on down to the cove – though it was terribly violated in the last century when they quarried the granite from it for the Thames Embankment. Lamorna has the reputation of being a painter's paradise, but I think it is too pretty to need painting.

You *could* then drive up the lane by the mill behind the pub (which is rather daring), or, safer, retrace your route to the main road. Either way you are back on B3315 and headed towards Newlyn and Penzance. You could even, outside the holiday season, take one of the right-hand turnings down to Mousehole (pronounced Mowzle by the common people, and said by scholars to mean 'maiden's estuary'; but quite obviously named after a local cave like a mouse's hole). Although Mousehole is a jolly little place and even puts an illuminated sea-serpent in the harbour at Christmas, it is also a dreadful place for getting jammed with your car. It is frankly better approached from the Newlyn side. But if you do venture in through the village of Paul (which is actually Mousehole's churchtown) you may see in the churchyard wall the monument to Dolly Pentreath erected in 1860 by, curiously, Prince Lucien Bonaparte.

Whether you drive on through Mousehole or have kept to the B3315 which brings you down a steep hill, you will arrive in Newlyn. Where Mousehole is a St Ives *manqué*, Newlyn is literally a different kettle of fish. Or rather fish at one end and Amalgamated Roadstone at the other: either way, it is a hardworking port and there are encouraging plans to develop it further. I say encouraging because there has to be somewhere where Cornishmen can find something more than hanging out Bed and Breakfast signs, and even if Newlyn is not picturesque it is genuine and businesslike and not, I think, offensive. Just near the central crossroads, opposite the Victorian church, there are warehouses selling freshly caught fish, smoked mackerel, and crabs and lobsters; and actually on the crossroads, a good and amazingly cheap fish and chip shop.

Newlyn's chief claim to the history books is that in July 1595 it was burnt by a raiding party of two hundred Spaniards, landed, I suppose, to exact revenge for the defeat of Armada and the activities of Cornish pirates. They destroyed much of Paul, Mousehole and Penzance as well, the inhabitants fleeing at the memory of an ancient prophecy that forecast –

There shall land on the rock of Merlin
Those who'll burn Paul Church, Penzance and Newlyn,

– for it is said the Spaniards did land at a point called Merlin's Rock, just south of Mousehole.

Newlyn has had its up and downs since then. Its fishery has always been at the mercy of overfishing and the competition of bigger boats from abroad or up-country: in 1896 the New-lyners boarded some Lowestoft and Yarmouth boats that had been fishing on Sundays and tipped all their catches back in the sea. To hear them talk today, it is a wonder they don't offer the same treatment to the Eastern Europe factory ships that suck up their mackerel by the millions in the Western approaches. But Newlyn does not look as if it had much to complain about, with brand new wharves and auction sheds, and a steady traffic in freezer trucks up-country and to the continent.

Newlyn cannot always have looked as plain as it does now, though if it was ever picturesque it was also exceedingly insanitary and constantly threatened with decimation by pesti-lence. But perhaps it was the fisherfolk and their boats, rather than their sanitation, that attracted Stanhope Forbes, Frank Bramley and the other founders of the Newlyn School, towards the end of the last century. And today, if St Ives can boast of Patrick Heron, Newlyn has Terry Frost perched high up on the hillside.

And so, at last, you may drive on along the seafront into Penzance, where there is a huge municipal car park adjoining the harbour. Penzance could offer hot and cold sea-water bathing as early as 1830, venturing to hope that 'the time is not far distant when this place will become a favourite resort of Hygieia and will supersede those numerous *watering* places which derive their fame alone from the caprice of fashion or popular prejudice, and which have nothing to recommend them but the eulogiums of visitants who cannot possibly appreciate their peculiar claims to merit.' This particular eulo-gium was addressed to invalids, but I am not sure that Hygieia would have been impressed. At the time the average age of death in Penzance was only 29, compared with a ripe 43 at Liskeard, at the eastern end of Cornwall.

But the holiday business did catch on with the arrival of the railway. An enormous train of 84 carriages puffed into Penzance one August day in 1855 and, before long, horse buses were connecting with the trains to ferry excursionists to the Logan Rock and Land's End. At first, there were complaints about rapacious Cornish landladies, but competition sorted that out, and Penzance has been known ever since as a very respectable place in which to holiday.

Betjeman rightly calls it a well-balanced town. West of Hayle River it is where you go for any substantial shopping, to get glass cut, a saddle mended, a bicycle repaired, or a new mantle for a Tilley lamp or a sack of pony nuts. It is where you find a doctor, a lawyer, a vet, a bank manager, architect, auctioneer or estate agent. It has schools and a hospital, a police station, the friendliest of railway stations, a public library and an early nineteenth-century private subscription library, a mysterious Jewish burial ground (though there is no Jewish community now nearer than Plymouth) and the council offices too.

The most useful shopping street, especially for food, is Causewayhead, lately made into a thoroughfare for pedestrians only (though this does not seem to mean much to local drivers). Among other things it contains one of the bakers for which Penzance ought to be famous. The official main street – Market Jew Street (which almost certainly derives from the Cornish 'Thursday Market' and has nothing to do with romances about Jewish or Phoenician tin-traders) – has a real character. The raised sidewalk with its rails and steps has a harbour-like appearance; and the domed classical market house at the top, with a statue of Humphry Davy in front of it, is the focal point of the town. Nor is Penzance without its intriguing, private corners. There is Victoria Square, off Bread Street; the bizarre Egyptian House in Chapel Street; and the nooks around the old Abbey Hotel near by.

You can see that I love Penzance; and yet I fear for it too. For out on the Eastern Green, on the town's approaches, are already squatting the great hangars of the Do-It-Yourself and Supermarket emporia, and they spell death to the small shopkeepers who have been the making of Penzance hitherto.

Already you can see the leprosy of shop closure in Market Jew Street.

To complete the loop we have made around the peninsula, you drive out past the Helicopter Port and go off at the roundabout for the few miles across country to the Hayle estuary. Going the other way, into Penzance, you now have the choice of bypassing it altogether and whizzing out to St Just or Land's End as if Penzance never existed. It seems to me a most unnecessary use of concrete and gravel, but apparently the Common Market had money to spare and so if you wish to be disappointed by Land's End ten minutes earlier than used to be the case, you can.

I would sooner stay to explore more of the back lanes we have passed by. There is the quiet, useful B3311 that runs from the eastern end of Penzance up to Zennor. There is the handy, wriggling lane from St Buryan to Crows-an-wra (which means 'Cross of the Witch'). There is the secret valley above Crowlas. And there is a special favourite that runs round the back of Rosewall Hill from the top of St Ives Hill to Towednack. After twenty years' exploring, there are still lanes I have never been down. To roll gently through them in the summer, with wildflower-scented air coming *whit-whit-whit* through the window, is real balm.

Giants in Those Days

In almost every mythology the giants come first; even before the gods – for they built the landscape.

Beside the road that leads from the Hayle estuary towards Halsetown, at the foot of Trencrom Hill, stands a large domed boulder. It is marked on the map as the Bowl Rock. The explanation is simple: giants used to live on the hill and amused themselves in a variety of energetic ways, notably by pitching stones at St Michael's Mount four miles away. They also played bowls, and this is one of them that rolled down the hill and got lost in the long grass by the stream.

Follow a side lane to the shoulder of the hill which, like the Bowl itself, is under the protection of the National Trust, and you will appreciate the likelihood of the story. The granite outcrops on the summit have been crudely linked together to form a rampart, and who else could have built such a fort but people of gigantic strength? According to Hunt's informants, the Trencrom giants were a cruel tribe who dragged their victims up the hill and slaughtered them on the flat rocks there, whose hollows and channels served to catch the blood.

The giants were also known to prey upon one another. One of them, with his lady, occupied the superb cliff castle that includes the Logan Rock, while down below in a cave lived a handsome young giant. As the old one lay snoozing in his granite chair, the young rival crept up on him, knifed him in the belly, tipped his carcase in the sea and took possession of the castle and the not-unwilling giantess.

Not all giants were so ill-disposed to each other. At one time the giant of St Michael's Mount and his colleague on Trencrom were friends to the point of sharing the same hammer, which they used to toss to one another across the bay when it was shouted for. The friendship ended when the hammer hit the Mount giant's wife and killed her.

Carn Galver, the hill which overlooks the road from Zennor to Morvah, was occupied by a giant named Holiburn, who was unusual in being well-disposed towards humans; though he expected them to keep up a steady supply of sheep and oxen for his dinner. In return he protected them against the Trencrom giants. Holiburn, too, was playful. But it is said his efforts to join in human sports ended in disaster when he patted the head of a young man from Chun, in congratulation for a particularly good quoit-throw, and shattered his skull. Holiburn pined with remorse and was dead in seven years. The heights and downs, like the Logan Rock castle, are crowded with stones that used to be described as the Giant's Chair or the Giant's Table or Wash-basin. I have noticed, however, that over the past fifty years Penwithians have lost interest in the specific names that the guides once used to emphasize. Come to that, there aren't the guides about that once there were, and perhaps they were the last survivors of the Droll-tellers.

From time to time in old pamphlets you read of gigantic skeletons being dug up here or there. They were probably animal bones; for there is no archaeological evidence anywhere in the world for the existence of a true race of giants. A small Mediterranean people might have been cowed by the arrival of a tall Celtic race, and later have fantasized them into giants. The fragments of pottery which have been found at some of the castles suggest a date of about 250–200 B.C., right for the Celts; and the emphasis on sport (including hammer throwing) and occasional human sacrifice sounds Celtic too. But whoever they were, their stature as giants must have been due more to their terrible reputations than to their actual physique.

Were there real people behind some of these legendary disguises? I am inclined to follow the approach of Sir Robert Birley to the supposed fable of Alfred and the cakes, and ask: Why should anyone have made up that particular story if it was not essentially true? Isn't it quite possible that one Celtic chieftain killed the wife of another during a hammer-throwing contest? Or that the Trencrom settlement was particularly devoted to human sacrifice? Or that the Logan Rock chieftain was murdered by his wife's lover? Or that the indigenous folk of Morvah paid protection money to a relatively benevolent chieftain on Carn Galver, and even that he killed one of them at some boisterous Celtic game? These are altogether more dependent upon something real having happened some time than are the names given to hunks of stone.

Still, if there was one piece of evidence to convince later generations that the giants really had been enormous, it must have been hunks of stone. Not so much the chairs and washbowls as the castle walls and the huge granite chambers that look like giant tables and are known as dolmens, cromlechs or (in Penwith) quoits: Zennor Quoit, Mulfra Quoit, Lanyon and Chun Quoits. Seen as they are now they do not readily suggest the tombs or sanctuaries they must once have been. The earth that was piled over them has blown away, and all you can see is a draughty box that might once have been used as a table or stool by somebody huge, huge enough to have assembled the granite blocks singlehanded.

The Cornish might have argued that there was no real reason why the ramparts at Trencrom, or the more polished examples at Chun and Castel-an-Dinas could only have been built by a giant. They themselves were constantly clearing rocks off their fields and piling them into stone hedges. (Today, with mechanical diggers and bulldozers, they are at it again – moving the hitherto immovable and tearing down hedges to merge small fields into big ones.) But the big hill-forts must have been constructed by fair-sized military forces, not scattered peasant farmers; and, above all, it must have taken more than the average country skills to put the quoits together. In fact the quoits, like the stone circles, are enormously older than the hill-forts and must have been constructed by pre-Celtic peoples. But to the mediaeval Cornish peasant of the lower farmlands they must all have seemed part of something done on the moors long ago, and by whom else but giants?

My favourite giant tale, one that appears in both Hunt's and Bottrell's collections, with variations, concerns a young carter called Tom and the giant Denbras. Denbras is simply

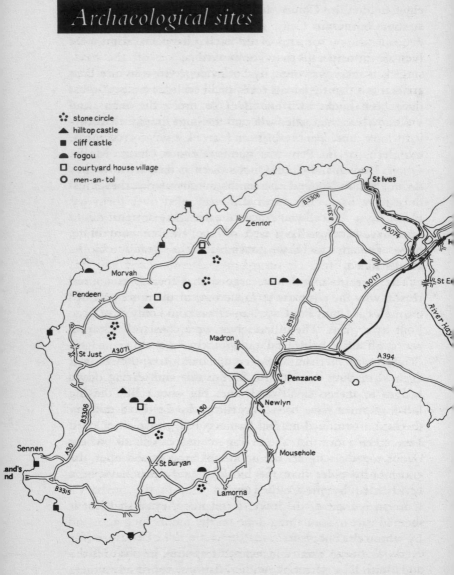

Archaeological sites

- **∴** stone circle
- **▲** hilltop castle
- **■** cliff castle
- **◗** fogou
- **□** courtyard house village
- **○** men-an-tol

St Ives

B3306
B3311
A3074

Zennor

St E

River Hay

Morvah

Pendeen

St Just
A3071

B3311

Madron

A394

Penzance

Newlyn

B3306

A30

Sennen
A30

and's
nd
B3315

St Buryan

Mousehole

Lamorna

Cornish for 'Big Fellow' and there is some hint that Tom was a giant, too, although Bottrell says he was 'no more than eight feet high' at a time when 'men in general were twice the size they are now'.

Tom was given a load of ale to take from Marazion to St Ives. The story tells how he heaved a tree off the road, singlehanded, somewhere by Ludgvan or Crowlas and then arrived at a point where the giant had built his hedges across the highway. Incensed at this, Tom drove his oxen clean through the barred gates and clattered into the giant's court-yard. Out came Denbras, fifteen feet tall, tore up an elm tree five feet taller and vowed he would teach the carter a lesson. Tom overturned his waggon, removed the axle with a wheel at one end, and defended himself without much trouble, for the giant was fat and out of condition.

The fight was conducted according to the best traditions of fair play, and at first Tom used only the wheel to ward off the blows. But after a while he got bored and decided to tickle the giant's ribs a little. He turned the axle round and gave his opponent a poke with the sharp end. The axle punctured Denbras's belly, the giant pitched forward and rammed it out through his back. Tom was heartbroken to hear his moans. Tom pulled the weapon out, plugged up the wounds with turf and tried to revive Denbras with a barrel of ale.

'It's no use, my son,' groaned the giant, 'I fear I shall kick the bucket. But I love thee for thy fair play, and all the copper and tin in my castle is thine.' Then the giant told Tom the secret names of his two dogs (Catchem and Tearem according to Hunt – Standby and Holdfast according to Bottrell) and Tom helped him up to the top of the castle hill, where Denbras could look his last upon his kingdom and upon the graves of his many wives, for he had the reputation of being a Bluebeard. There he breathed his last.

There is a great deal more to the story, but I shall cut it short.

Tom acquires a wife, finds the castle full of treasure (for everyone knows that all giants had treasure); he conjures the dogs with their secret names and has a series of adventures with a tinker called Jack. Jack is almost as good a sportsman as

Tom. I suspect he may stand for 'Cousin Jack', the typical Cornishman. Be that as it may, he is eventually allowed to marry Tom's eldest daughter, Genevra. The couple set up house at Chun (the site of yet another hilltop castle), and so the tale rambles happily on.

It seems to me that here we have yet another memory of the Celtic hilltop barons, their enmities and alliances. But we have something more specific, too. For if you take the road from Marazion towards St Ives by way of Ludgvan and Crowlas, it runs on towards a straggle of cottages called – of all things – 'Castle Gate'. There appears to be no such thing as a castle in sight, but overlooking the road is the hill marked on the map 'Castel-an-Dinas'.

On the top of the hill are two extraordinary features, if not three. The third is the huge crater of the roadstone quarry; but the other two are a folly called Roger's Tower, built about 1800 A.D., and behind it a circular Iron Age Fort dated about 200–300 B.C. The view from it conjures up the prospect of a very tidy little kingdom indeed. But I have not been able to locate the graves of the giant queens.

Nor, unfortunately, have I been able to find the grave of the eccentric Mr James Hosken of Ludgvan who quarrelled with the Church and declined to be buried in consecrated ground. Instead, he was interred one day in 1823 'near the ruins of an ancient tower called Castle Dennis', lying between two inscriptions that read 'Custom is the idol of fools' and 'Virtue only consecrates the ground'. The burial was presided over by a Baptist minister from Penzance, and five thousand people came to stare.

The story does not end there, for more than a century later the grave was encroached upon by quarrying operations and some Hosken relatives offered him sanctuary in a quiet corner of Saltash at the opposite extreme of the Duchy. But nor is this all, for in a field below Ding Dong, about three miles from Castle Gate, is an empty grave with exactly the same two epitaphs on it; and it belongs to a redoubtable old atheist called Benny Shedford who must have been a later admirer of Hosken. Apparently local disapproval prevented him from being buried in his intended tomb, and he was put away at St

Just graveyard 'where the old men belong to piss after the sermon'.

If you wish to inspect the castle and Roger's folly, take the signposted road to the quarry, off the B3311, and when you reach the works entrance follow the track to the left of it, which should be marked 'footpath'. You must take the greatest care to obey any warnings about blasting operations, and keep well away from the edge of the crater. It is a fearful place – enough to make the giants of old feel inadequate.

And yet I still prefer their works to the works of man. You can see more of them by taking the small road that runs from Morvah to Madron and Penzance. About half-way along on the eastern side of it, there is the celebrated Lanyon Quoit, one of the most photographed of its kind – and the least authentic, for it stands upon only three legs, one of which is clearly at the wrong angle. In fact the original chamber collapsed during a gale on the night of 19 October 1815; it seems strange that a mere gale should have upset it, but the story is that somebody had been digging round it in the hopes of uncarthing the treasure of the giant of St Michael's Mount, whose tomb it was supposed to be. Nine years later, the monument was restored by Captain Giddy and Lieutenant Goldsmith RN, using tackle and sheer-legs from Plymouth dockyard; and finding one of the blocks of granite broken, they did the best they could with what was left.

A digression here on the name of Lieutenant Goldsmith, who evidently felt an obligation towards ancient monuments, following an earlier escapade involving the Logan Rock at Treen. Logan rocks are supposed to 'log' or sway when pushed, and the Treen boulder was a particularly spectacular example. The local people, who made tips from visitors by showing it off, vowed that no matter how much it swayed no power on earth could ever dislodge it. Goldsmith determined to prove them wrong. He brought ashore the crew of his revenue cutter, the *Nimble*, and levered the boulder off its perch, whence it crashed onto the turf below. A great outcry ensued, especially from the deprived villagers of Treen. The lieutenant was ordered by the Admiralty to replace the rock at his own expense, which he did with the aid of the equipment from Plymouth and much refreshment of the local labour-force: you can still purchase copies of the accounts. There is something altogether fishy about the whole thing, and I suspect that something is connected with smuggling. For while Goldsmith and his merry men were overthowing the Logan stone a large cargo of French brandy was being landed at the cove round the corner. Be that as it may, it is my opinion, however hard subsequent generations of guides have tried to persuade me otherwise, that the Logan has never rocked since. I know two that do: one on Zennor Hill, one in the grounds of the Eagle's Nest.

But to get back on to the Morvah to Madron road: there is a turning off it to the west that is clearly marked 'Chun Castle', and I recommend following it. Chun, you will recall, was where Jack the tinker (sometimes called 'Jack the Hammer') settled with Genevra, raised a family, found no end of tin and fought off the red-headed raiders who, according to Bottrell, landed at Pendeen, Porthmeor and Pendower. The castle today lies in two distinct concentric circles, all bashed and battered by robberies for building stone. Only a century ago the walls were still twelve feet high, and earlier still it must have been a formidable sight. Within the ramparts are a stuffed well and outlines of a series of chambers built by mediaeval squatters.

Chun has a superb view. You can see the sea on both sides of the peninsula, and look south-westwards towards Land's End with its radio pylons, and the mysterious heap of Carn Kenidjack. In August the smell of heather honey is almost overpowering, and the heather turf is flecked with the rich scrambled-egg of dwarf gorse. A few hundred yards west of the castle is Chun Quoit, small but undamaged and really a better example of what quoits were about than Lanyon.

If the ancient Cornish were convinced that castles and quoits were the work of giants, they had quite different ideas about those other inhabitants of the moors, the circles and standing stones. This is curious at first sight, because you might have thought that both could be explained as belonging to one or other of the giants' games. That they were not so explained is accounted for, I suggest, by the survival of a very

ABOVE: *St Ives harbour*
BELOW: *Botallack, minehead*

LEFT: *Sancreed, Celtic cross*
ABOVE: *Lamorna, the mill*
BELOW: *St Levan church*

RIGHT: *Pednevounder beach*
BELOW: *Kenegie Home Farm*

LEFT: *Gurnard's Head, ruined engine-house*

ABOVE: *Greenburrow, ruined engine-house*

BELOW: *Botallack, ruined smelter*

ABOVE: *Penberth, fishing boats*

BELOW: *Penberth cove*

LEFT: *Madron Baptistry, the font*
ABOVE: *Madron Well, prayer rags at the Wishing Well*
BELOW: *Carn Kenidjack, the haunted hill*
OPPOSITE ABOVE: *Tresco, Cromwell's Castle*
OPPOSITE BELOW: *Tresco, the Blockhouse*

ABOVE: *Sea pinks*
BELOW: *Wild rhododendrons*

powerful folk tradition that their purposes were totally different, that they were in fact magical, even if nobody could recall the precise details of their use.

There are about a dozen stone circles in Penwith, and maybe more lying tumbled in the bracken or hard to recognize because those stones which could be readily moved have been carted off for gateposts (some quite recently). I suspect this is even more true of the standing stones, several of which have been incorporated into hedges or been explained away as 'scratching posts for cattle'.

Of the circles, three are major examples for this part of the world – the Merry Maidens, beside the B3315, near the Lamorna turning; Boscawen-Un, much harder to find in the fields north of St Buryan; and the Nine Maidens, which are on the moors near the old Ding Dong mine, behind Carn Galver.

The word 'Maiden' is probably a confusion of the Cornish 'Maen', meaning 'Stone'. 'Maen' also gets confused with 'Men', and the Merry Maidens are also known as 'Dawns Men', which is really nothing to do with people observing the rising sun but means 'Stone Dance'. This is a good deal more significant in the light of the most popular of legendary explanations, that these are petrified dancers (maidens, of course) turned to stone for dancing on Sunday. It is usual to ascribe this fearful warning to Puritan preachers, who also interpreted the nearby standing stones as 'Pipers' or 'the Blind Fiddler' similarly punished for providing the music. But there were periods in the Middle Ages that were equally stern about keeping the Sabbath, and I think the legends are much older than the sixteenth or seventeenth centuries.

They may, indeed, have reflected something essentially true, that the circles really were dancing places. There are circles elsewhere in Britain where an outer circuit has been trampled hard, as if by dancing feet, and although we cannot assume that every tribe and region used its circles for identical purposes, ritual dancing is a characteristic of most tribal societies and the more you think about it, the more surprising it would be if dancing did *not* go on round such circles.

According to the authoritative Aubrey Burl, more than 900

circles have been recorded in the British Isles. This number may come as a shock, but they are all recorded to the west of a line between Newcastle and Southampton with thick clusters in areas like counties Cork and Tyrone in Ireland, Aberdeenshire and the islands of Lewis and Arran, the Lake District and the Peak District, and Dartmoor. Stonehenge notwithstanding, it is easiest to make your stone circle where there is stone. The wooden circles, of which there must have been many, have long ago perished.

So far as radiocarbon dating has been applied to the remains found in them, circle building seems to have gone on between 3300 B.C. and 1500 B.C. The Penwith circles are relatively small and simple specimens and were probably built in the middle-to-later period, say 2500–2000 B.C. It is extremely hard to be sure about dates, largely because of the rarity of any finds associated with them. They do not seem to have been burial places, no treasure has been found under the pillars, and there is no evidence of animal or human sacrifices or (a theory of mine for a time) of the circles being used as market places.

So what *were* they for? Here a host of half-scientific, half-crackpot theories crowd in, and almost every one meets with angry objections from some other camp. The question of megalithic alignments, for example – the lining up of one site with others – is so esoteric and so liable to juggling, so hard, also, to credit to the minds of megalithic surveyors, that it is best left alone in these pages. Elaborate constructions have been made using hypothetical units of measurement, supposed underground streams or magnetic forces which would explain the circles as focal points or pulses of earth forces. More reputable theories have been published explaining the circles as astronomical observatories, or more trendily 'computers', and there is no doubt that some of them at least would have forecast the turning of the seasons in a way that was of value to farming or herding peoples. It has even been suggested that the Celts were preceded by an ancient race of scholar-priests who understood Pythagoras and practised a religion that linked astronomy and agriculture.

Even today farmers are at the mercy of natural forces they

cannot control. Ancient man was even more at their mercy since he could not properly understand them, either. But he strove constantly to do so, and must have become convinced that by the use of sympathetic magic he could at least influence and appease those forces, assure them of his respect and gratitude and fear. Forces, however, is too impersonal a word. The whole of ancient mythology is an attempt to *personalize* nature, beginning with the Earth Mother and the Heaven Father, whose spirits met and coupled and who had countless minor relatives and attendants in the skies and seas, forests, streams, none of whom the prudent man dared ignore.

The stone circles, however, do not seem to be related to local objects of veneration. They are set high up in the open, like miniature horizons of Earth lying exposed to Heaven, and when the antiquarians of the seventeenth and eighteenth centuries described them as the temples of the Druids – even though Druids were a late, Celtic caste – they were probably not far wrong. We do not know how the circles may have been draped or dressed or screened with hurdles or skins. It is possible that mysteries were prepared or conducted within them, while the common folk gathered outside or processed round. We should beware of assuming that because they look primitive today, only the simplest of cults could have been connected with them. The megalithic peoples did not write, but there is reason to believe that their priests or shamans spent a lifetime memorizing and passing on the most elaborate myths, rules and rituals; so that their religion may have been much more sophisticated than we are prepared to grant today.

Even so, when every other period of history has found Cornwall frankly primitive and backward, I find it hard to believe that Penwith can ever have been an advanced centre of animistic theology. I find it hard, for example, to avoid the conclusion that the chambered tombs – of which the quoits are the surviving cores – were regarded as earth-wombs, to which the dead had ultimately to return; or that some at least of the standing-stones were not phallic symbols (there are some in Ireland, not to mention Greece and India, with nicely rounded tops to them). Nothing especially subtle about that, and if you wish to imagine the circles as sites for tribal orgies, there is some support for that in the form of traditions that the Devil (the horned god of the herds) used to couple there with the witches of Penwith. More sympathetic magic.

As astronomical computers, the Penwith circles do not appear very advanced. Like others in Cornwall, they tend to have their tallest single stone at WSW, which might indicate sunset at the beginning of Spring and the end of Autumn but would not help with the equinoxes. There is certainly no standard model of British circle, or even of Cornish. On Bodmin Moor and Dartmoor the stones tend to number 28 or 30; in Penwith they are down to 18 or 20, though it is often hard to tell how many have been stolen. There is some suspicion that the Nine Maidens (of whom I counted eleven) are not really a circle at all but the remains of an enclosure sheltering Iron Age huts. In any case, they are a sloppy lot, tumbling all over the place among the heather and the tawny-tailed grass. Boscawen-Un has been restored, though you might not believe it from the gorse all around, and has an intriguing tilted stone in the middle. Again, what is it for? Nobody can suggest an astronomical use for it and nothing has been found buried at its foot, nor is it the usual thing for circles in Penwith to have such a focus.

Single stones present a whole new range of possibilities. There are three or four in Penwith with crude Latin inscriptions that mark them clearly as tombstones. There is one inside St Just church reading SELUS IC IACIT (accompanied by a Chi-Rho) which has been guessed to be the epitaph of St Levan. There is another, rarely seen specimen by a stream near Gulval, that reads (in translation) 'Here is the grave of Quentaucus son of Dinuus'. And the best known, marked not far from Lanyon Quoit as Men Scryfa (Written Stone), translates 'Grave of Rialobran son of Cunoval'. These may be of the fifth or sixth centuries, and there are others not inscribed that are grave monuments and at whose feet urns of ashes have been found.

But there are others again which have yielded nothing and must have served some other purpose. The fact that a stone must have served some other purpose. The fact that a stone like the Men Scryfa (sometimes Scryfys) stands alone in a field and is neither part of a cemetery nor on a commanding height suggests to me that Rialobran (The Royal Raven) may have been buried where he was slain in battle, and that other stones may also be battle monuments. There is a recorded tradition that the two tall 'Pipers' across the road from the Merry Maidens mark either the positions of the two commanders during the battle between Athelstan and the last of the independent Cornish or are Peace Stones erected to perpetuate the treaty between them. They remind me eerily of the tall pillar-stone to which Cuchulainn, the Hound of Ulster, bound himself in his death agony, and which he split with his passing sigh. There is something lonely, heroic and defiant about such stones, something which Barbara Hepworth sensed and reflected in her figures.

A mile north of Lanyon Quoit, near the Men Scryfa, down a rough track that begins opposite an 1882 school-house, stands one of the most curious of Penwith curiosities, the Men-an-Tol, or Stone-of-the-Hole. It consists of an upright slab with a large porthole, and a stone pillar looking through it from either side. The whole arrangement is oddly low-down and wrong-looking, too much a deliberate piece of abstract sculpture and not enough an instrument of mystery. Still, I must be wrong, for it had the reputation of curing scrofula in children when they were passed three times through it naked. Possibly it used to be part of a vanished tomb and was transposed to its present position in quite recent times: I suspect Lieutenant Goldsmith again. As the entrance to a chamber tomb it would certainly have been significantly genital – as it is now, it points towards nothing of any meaning and foreign tourists photograph their girl-friends smiling through it.

Which leaves me with the one feature of this giant-and-Druid-haunted landscape that may be even more curious: the fogous (pronounced 'foogoos'), a name derived from the Cornish for 'caves'. A fogou is a most mysterious thing, but if there had been aircraft in those days you would have said without hesitation that it was a Stone Age air-raid shelter, for underground passage – one end having the appearance of a main entrance and the other of an emergency exit – and opening off the passage is a circular chamber. The most easily inspected fogou forms an annexe to the Iron Age village at Carn Euny, a Department of the Environment site a mile west of Sancreed. This has a most satisfying passage to creep along. There is a more disappointing fogou at the other preserved village site, Chysauster, between Nancledra and Newmill; and a fine but private place in the gardens of Crosbie Garstin's old home at the top of the Lamorna valley.

There is an alleged fogou which I have seen but do not believe in attached to another ruined settlement at Porthmeor in Zennor parish, and others that I believe in but cannot find. But my own favourite fogou is the one at Pendeen Manor – childhood home of the illustrious eighteenth-century anti-quarian Borlase. You may find it by turning right as you enter Pendeen from St Ives, down the turning to Pendeen lighthouse, and looking for a track that forks to the right towards the grey manor. You should park out of the way of farmyard traffic and ask round the back of the house, or in the cowshed, for permission and guidance to the fogou (which is cheerfully given).

Pendeen fogou is virtually *part* of the farmyard. The last time I was there it was piled high with old motor-car tyres which had been weighting down the covers on the silage heap. The emergency exit had a fine view into a pool of cow sludge – all very typical of the way the Cornish decline to grant any special privileges to pre-history, and expect antiquities and rusty junk to coexist. This fogou looks more like a thick stone wall from the outside, and I wonder if it was ever completely earthed over. Inside it is creepy, especially if you have forgotten to bring a torch, and the chamber off the passage is difficult to squeeze into over the age of about fifty.

If the problem of the circles is that they resemble nothing we have any use for today, the problem of the fogous is that they resemble too many. A shelter or refuge of some kind – if not against air raids? But surely the stupidest kind of hidey-hole, far too easily starved out, smoked out or blocked up by raiders. A storage centre? But why put things underground, where they would rot and grow mouldy? A tomb? But these people seem to have used other ways to dispose of their dead, and if the fogous were communal charnel houses, no bones have been found in them, nor traces of ashes.

Personally, I am inclined to attribute some magical-religious purpose to them. Perhaps I have a Freud-infected mind, but there is an obvious parallel with the womb and birth-channel in the fogou, even though that does not explain the two entrances. At any rate you can imagine people climbing in at one end, crouching in the chamber for whatever ritual may have been practised, and then emerging reborn or initiated at the other. So a fogou may have been a temple of some kind, or at least a holy place, which might account for the fact that by no means all of them, as at Pendeen, seem to be associated with settlements.

Can the legends help us? Not much, but there is one reference to fogous in a story we shall meet later, concerning Duffy and the Devil. The relevant point here is that, once again, the Devil was seen consorting with his witches, in 'a Fugoe Hole'. The tale as Hunt records it says that he 'kicked them' soundly, but it may well have been a coarser word, and we may be back with fertility rites. It is all sheer guesswork. Once again, the crudeness of whatever life was led there has deprived us of the artefacts or carvings left by more obliging cultures. All the more room for imagination.

Sacred and Profane

Cornwall competes with Ireland as a land of saints, and their names are almost as musical as the names of the Cornish places with which they merge. There is St Enoder and St Erney and St Erme; St Breock and St Clether and St Erth; St Ludgvan and St Breward; St Blazey and St Day; St Eval and St Gennys and St Wenn; St Tudy and St Veep; St Nectan and St Teath; St Piran and St Pinnock and St Minver and St Merryn; St Mabyn and St Mellion; St Mewan and St Endellion; St Neot and St Levan; St Issey and St Buryan, and half a calendar more whom you will hardly find anywhere else in Britain.

Some of them are, in fact, Roman saints misnamed. St Erme is St Hermes and St Erney is St Terninus, and the wickedly named St Eval is actually dedicated to St Uvelus. Not that those names ring any louder a bell in one's mind than their Cornish corruptions.

West of Hayle River, the parish churches are almost all Celtic dedications, for Cornwall as a whole was part of the loose confederation of the Celtic Church, which claims to have survived the Roman withdrawal and to be older in these islands than St Augustine's importation.

I must confess to a sentimental fondness for the Celtic Church and wish I knew more about it; though I might like it less if I did. In fact, nobody seems to know very much about it. The Celtic Church was essentially a monkish institution, closer in some ways to Constantinople than to Rome. Missionaries fanned out from the abbeys and priories, setting up their solitary cells, preaching, baptizing and healing among the people, in the manner of early apostles. They conducted a Communion Service which has been compared to the Church of England's Series Two, they practised the washing of feet (which has been oddly dropped from the western liturgy), they encouraged lusty congregational singing, and they celebrated Easter on the wrong day to Rome's way of thinking. The clergy also offended Rome by shaving the front of their scalps instead of the top. Their way of life was simple and hard, and they themselves were individualists to the point of eccentricity. At first, we seldom hear of any bishop disciplining them, though discipline must have developed as the original missionaries made converts and the single 'lan' or cell grew into a colony. Alas, the Celtic Church was hardly organized to take on Rome with its centralized organization, its hierarchies and its alliances with the state. The Anglo-Saxon Kingdom of Northumbria turned to Rome in 664 A.D. and the twilight of the Celtic Church set in. Athelstan's conquest of Cornwall must have settled matters here, though some Celtic practices lingered on into Norman times. One thing the Celtic Church bequeathed to posterity – the square-ended parish church with an east window to let in the rising sun, instead of the semicircular apse of the Roman basilica. You can see the origin of this in, for example, the little baptistry of St Maddern in Madron parish – the object of one of the short walks described in my final chapter.

You can see another 'square end' not far from the parish church of Sancreed, and although the church leaflet gives it a rather perfunctory note, I find this little chapel peculiarly thrilling. In a moment, I shall relate how to find it. Sancreed itself is a most charming backwater, with five ancient crosses in the churchyard and a loud rookery behind the church tower. The rectory has become an artists' colony, and used to produce some distinguished pottery among other work; and the old Bird-in-Hand Inn across the road from the church has long been a private home (more's the pity). The church of St Sancredus was presumably dedicated to one of two possible Saint Credans. One was a disciple of St Petrock, a fairly far-flung saint found outside Cornwall; but the other was an Irishman who, according to legend, accidentally killed his father and, out of remorse, became a swineherd, living so exemplary a life that he was accounted a saint. Once again, why not? There is a certain supporting tradition in the fact that Sancreed was long famous for its pigs, although a practical explanation may be that – since it was one of the few parishes in Penwith without a sea-coast – it was about the only one where the pork did not taste of fish offal.

To find the chapel ruins, you cross the farmyard behind the Bird-in-Hand and follow a line of electricity poles down a track. At the end of the track you fork right, over a stile with iron bars to it, up through the bracken past an ugly concrete water-tank, and then over a three-step stone stile on to a path that seems to lead down the middle of a hedge. Almost immediately you are in the chapel enclosure. It was cleared in 1908 at the expense of three lady visitors, and a replica Cornish cross erected with an inscription that reads: 'Of your charity pray for the sick, the sorrowful, the tempted, the sinning, the dying and those who rest in Christ'. The efforts to keep the site accessible were renewed in 1973 by Michael Shanks, in memory of his wife Juliet, and a slate tablet against the outer wall of the chapel touchingly records this.

The most intriguing thing about the place is that there is a holy well *underneath* the chapel. A flight of rough, mossy steps leads down to it, and in one corner of the chamber there are signs of an aperture opening into a trough that runs for several yards down the enclosure, beside the path that you have trodden. My own rather fanciful explanation of this is that there was once a baptistry or font here. The saint would pray loudly for holy water, and an assistant in the well-chamber would hear him and start ladling it down the trough – a miracle! Less romantically, it may only have been a way of providing a public water supply while keeping the women and their buckets from disturbing the peace of the chapel. And peaceful it is today. As the memorial to Juliet Shanks says: *La sua voluntate e nostra pace* – His Will is our Peace.

If St Credan really were here, it would have been about A.D. 580, but primitive constructions like these are almost impossible to date by themselves. Credan would have been a relatively late arrival in Penwith. St Erc (of St Erth) is supposed to have died in 514 at the age of 90; and since he arrived with his sister St Ia (of St Ives) and St Uny (of Uny

Lelant), there must have been a wave of incoming saints into the Hayle estuary from Ireland a good century before Credan. The modes of transport used by Celtic saints were often original. St Ia arrived on a leaf; St Kea floated from Ireland kneeling on a rock; and St Piran came on a millstone with which he had been cast into the sea by his enemies. Being interpreted less romantically, I take this to mean that the first came in a boat with a large green or brown sail, the second with a portable altar-stone, and the third either with his own grinding quern or else as an unwanted exile.

There is another simple chapel, known as Chapel Jane, on the cliff edge below the footpath just east of the Gurnard's Head. There is not much left of the walls and pottery finds suggest a date in the twelfth or thirteenth century, a good deal later than the age of saints, though it has been rebuilt at least twice. The cove below the site – Treen Cove, sometimes called Boat Cove – was used by a small seining fleet during the last century. You can still see the ruins of the pilchard shed where the fish were pressed and salted. Romance has it that fishermen used the chapel long ago to pray for fair weather or give thanks for a good catch. It would have been a steep climb, though, and I have a different speculation.

Chapel Jane is in Zennor parish. Until recently the only thing known about its patron, St Senara, was that *nothing* was known: until in 1924 an acquaintance of Robert Morton Nance ventured the interesting speculation that she might have been identical with Azenor, a sixth-century princess from Brittany and mother of St Budoc ('the Drowned One').

This is promising, for a start, since Celtic saints do tend to come in families. But the Breton legend of Azenor holds out even richer promise.

It is said that she was the daughter of the Count of Leon, wedded to the Count of Goello. One day Azenor was out hunting with her father, and had paused to cook their mid-day meal over a small fire, when a snake leapt out of the undergrowth and fastened its fangs upon the father's arm. Rapidly, Azenor anointed her breast with milk and oil and bared it to the serpent. The snake – knowing a good thing when it saw one – transferred its attentions to the Princess. As it did so, she seized her father's hunting knife, severed the breast and hurled it – snake attached – into the fire. Heaven was so impressed that it rewarded her with a breast of gold.

They returned home – to the inevitable jealous stepmother. Envious of Azenor's added attraction, the stepmother accused her of infidelity; with what evidence is unknown, but with sufficient pressure to have the noble girl condemned to be burnt alive. When it was discovered that Azenor was four months pregnant this sentence was altered to the less immediately fatal one of being nailed in a barrel and cast into the sea, so that her judges might escape the crime of murdering the unborn child.

Inside the tossing barrel an angel appeared to Azenor and fed her. After five months, a little boy was born and the barrel was soon washed up on the coast of Ireland, near Waterford. A passing kern saw the cask and, expecting liquor, was about to stave it in when a child's voice was heard, urging him to have a care. He did, and out stepped Azenor with the babe pressed to her golden breast. In due course Budoc grew to be abbot of Beau Port, near Waterford. Then follow two alternative versions of the tale. According to one, Budoc despaired of ever being able to civilize his barbarous flock and removed to Brittany floating in a stone coffin (like any good Celtic saint). According to the other version, Azenor's stepmother fell ill and, on her death-bed, confessed that she had fabricated the charges against the Princess. The Count of Goello sought her in one country after another, and at last found her in Ireland, together with her son. The Count set sail for Brittany with them but died on the way; and Azenor did not long survive him, though Budoc lived on to become Bishop of Dol and was finally canonized.

Now we know that passengers between Ireland and Brittany commonly sailed to the northern coast of Penwith, made the short but welcome journey overland and took a second ship from St Michael's Mount onward. We have also seen that there is a landing place to Treen Cove, though the coves closer to Zennor churchtown (as it now is) are inhospitable. What is more natural than that Azenor should have made this landfall and commemorated her dead husband by founding the little chapel on the clifftop? Chapel Jane? Perhaps his name was *Jean*. And if Azenor herself lingered on in the district and died there, that would account for the dedication of a church to her. Perhaps it is a pity that Zennor is now celebrated for its pagan mermaid, rather than for the Saint with the Golden Breast, who would have made a splendid piece of painted mediaeval woodcarving, babe at breast. At least it was a pleasant coincidence that the last incumbent, Canon Shane Cotter (to whom I am indebted for the legend), came, like Budoc, from Ireland.

If St Azenor's right to be here is something of a fantasy, there is no doubt about St Levan's. Whether he existed or not he has a parish firmly named after him; and a delightful place it is, in spite of its ancient reputation as a haven of witches. St Levan is more properly known as St Selevan, a form of Solomon, while he has also been identified with one 'Selyf', a brother of St Just and possibly the subject of the crude SELUS IC IACIT (Selus lies here) in St Just church. At any rate, he is also known in Brittany, which was colonized by the Cornish.

You find St Levan church by taking the Porthcurno turning off the B3315. Porthcurno is virtually a company cove, being the landfall of the old Eastern Telegraph Company cable, now Cable & Wireless, and a training school for its telegraphers. Nevertheless, there is a fine sandy beach and a convenient car park, both public. For St Levan, however, you ignore these and drive on up the hill to the right of the beach. This takes you past the entrance to the open air Minack Theatre, and bends round to the right. Just as you get a glimpse of the church, it is time to swerve hard right through a narrow entrance into the field where you should park your car. In the season, someone will arrive to collect a small fee: otherwise you drop it in a collecting tin, which is the least you can do for the convenience. There is very little space elsewhere.

The minute churchtown, which used to include an inn, is the very best sort of dead end. I think it possesses the best of the Penwith churches, its little battered tower covered from base to pinnacles with grey-green lichen, and the graveyard snuggled around it full of Angoves and Hoskens. The

fifteenth-century granite interior looks as if it had been carved
by the sea, as if the tide came in and out of the door, and the
pew-ends of the same period are full of character. They show
a shepherd, a jester in cap and bells, two mediaeval parishioners in profile, and a pilgrim off to Compostella with his
breviary and cockle-shell. One of them also depicts two fish,
eye to eye, as if on one hook, and this leads us straight into the
arms of St Levan himself.

If you take the path opposite the car park entrance, cross
the stream, climb up the hill a little and then turn left down
the valley, you will soon find yourself looking down on to
Porth Chapel where St Levan is said to have landed when
he came. His holy well and baptistry (looking not very
impressive) stand beside the path, and there are ancient
granite steps leading down to the ruins of his chapel. Water
from the well is still used occasionally for christenings,
though if I were an anxious mother I should see it was
boiled first.

According to Hunt, however, St Levan did not live near his
chapel, but at the top of the Porthcurno valley at a spot still
marked as Bodellan. From there he used to walk down the
valley, forking right along a path behind the former Porthcurno Hotel and across the fields to a farm called Rospletha.
You can still do the same yourself, though you may not be
able to confirm the claim that the grass grows greener where
the saint used to tread. From Rospletha the obvious thing to
do is to carry on to St Levan church: there is an old cross
beside the path and a stile in the churchyard wall with a coffin
stone to rest the casket on. One way or another, St Levan
made his way down towards the sea to fish. I believe he went
the churchyard way, for on the south side of the church is a
rock, cleft in two, upon which he used to sit and rest. The
legend tells us the saint clove it himself by striking it with his
fist and then prophesying:

> When with panniers astride
> A pack-horse can ride
> Through St Levan's stone,
> The world will be done.

I am not sure, but I cannot help feeling that the fissure *is* wider than it was forty years ago, and that a tall enough pack-horse *might* be able to squeeze through, one of these days.

But to return to St Levan's fishing and the significance of the pew-end: we are told that one evening St Levan was on his favourite rock with his hook baited and his line out. Suddenly he felt a strong jerk, and, pulling in, found two bream on the one hook. This seemed unnatural and unnecessary to the saint, who only needed enough for himself; but to avoid unfairness to either fish, he threw them both back. A moment later, the same thing happened. When the two fish bit the third time, St Levan acknowledged divine intervention and kept them both. On returning home to Bodellan, what should he find but that his sister, St Breage, had come to visit him with her two children. Doubtless blaming himself for not having fished still more, the saint assured her there was fish enough for everyone.

But the tale has a sting, or rather a choke, in it. The children were greedy, gobbled the fish, bones and all, and died of asphyxiation. Ever since when, we are told, the sea bream has been known as a 'choke-child' – though some insist it was the shad. Well, I have never caught shad near St Levan, but I have caught beautiful little sea bream, and all I can say is that they must have been exceedingly delicate children. As for St Levan's fishing rock, it is still there and a good place for pollock.

Nothing very holy, then, about St Levan. Just the odd curse or two, rather as a present-day Cornish vicar is liable to be remembered for his oddities rather than his sermons. Further east in Cornwall there is a fish story concerning St Neot, whose well contained three fishes, one of which he was allowed to eat every day, finding it miraculously replaced the following morning. One day – the saint being ill in bed – his servant extracted *two* fish and served them up cooked to his master, hoping to restore his strength. Instead of eating them, the saint prayed over his supper with great fervour and then ordered the servant to cast it into the well. This was done. Next morning the two cooked fish were found swimming happily with the other and routine was restored. I must say, if *I* had been furtively stocking a saint's well with trout, I should have been annoyed at having to haul out two grilled ones and find an extra live fish before morning.

St Neot, as it happens, was a midget about fifteen inches tall. There is no suggestion that St Levan or St Senara were anything but the normal height. But there is an area, centred on the figure of St Just, where the saints overlap the giants. I can only suppose this is because St Just is giant country, and anyone assuming importance there was liable to acquire the legends of the previous incumbent. St Just, for example, is said to have quarrelled for no good reason with his neighbour-missionary, St Sennen. One day, each of them tore up a massive boulder and hurled it at the other. The two rocks collided at the half-way point and fell to earth as Carn Brea (pronounced 'Bray'). Pure giantry. But there is a faint touch of religion in the story of St Just and St Keverne of the Lizard peninsula.

It is said that Just paid Keverne a visit, and that soon after Just had left, Keverne missed his favourite chalice. Correctly guessing that his guest had stolen it, St Keverne strode after him bawling the Celtic equivalent of 'Stop, thief!' The only effect it had was to speed up the massive stride of St Just, so that the only course open to St Keverne was the classic giant response of throwing stones. He threw them to such effect that St Just dropped the treasure in the heather – at which St Keverne contented himself by firing off his remaining stones and recovering the chalice from where it had fallen. How else can you account for that line of boulders known as the Crowza Stones, so out of keeping geologically with the surrounding countryside?

Penwith, it seems to me, is a profoundly religious country-side which has never really found its proper expression since the Celtic Church withered. Clearly it spoke to the condition of the Celtic and pre-Celtic peoples. And it offered countless nooks for the Irish, Welsh or Breton saints to plant their modest roots: small-scale, highly individual demesnes, friendly enough towards their neighbours, but each fiercely convinced that it alone was best.

It would be nice to believe that each of the dozens of stone crosses that punctuate the lanes of Penwith had been put there by an early Celtic saint. They have a crudeness about them that suggests the very earliest times, even if they lack the fine decoration of the Irish and Northumbrian crosses and even some of those further east in Cornwall. Yet, when the first missionaries arrived in Penwith, I doubt whether the skill was available to carve even the simplest crosses from the unyielding granite. Some of those in the lanes were put up as late as the fourteenth and fifteenth centuries, and most of them have some connection with parish boundaries dating from Saxon and Norman times. Others mark paths leading towards parish churches, a few could be explained as marking the site of a particular (but now forgotten) event, or may be adaptations of pagan standing-stones. But although the old Celtic chapels usually have a well nearby for baptisms, I cannot think of any in Penwith that has the symbol of crucifixion. Even allowing for the fact that crosses were knocked down and decapitated by anti-papist puritans, I am afraid we must abandon any idea of St Levan and the rest as great cross-builders.

Theirs was a less monumental church than that of Rome, and closer to nature. Communion with nature is very far from being the essence of Christianity: the religion we know today is literate, theologically complex and basically a city product. But if any religion is a true religion it must include two elements which the cities find hard to supply and which Penwith offers, if it offers the human spirit anything at all. The first is the setting for contemplation – detachment from business and luxury, confrontation with something over and above the human scramble. The second is the vast rhythms of the tide and the seasons that cannot be tinkered with by man, and to which the Celtic saints with their fishing and farming and sailing had to come to terms. But they, of course, were dealing with a whole people much closer to nature than we are today.

Penwith now, like Berwick-upon-Tweed or Hemel Hempstead, is what it is fashionable to call 'a post-Christian society'; though I wonder if it would not be more to the point to call it, rather, 'post-Church'. The Anglican parishes survive, serving at least a social function, often combined together like Zennor-with-Towednack or Madron-with-Morvah, but they are scarcely power-houses of spiritual fervour. The Methodists have closed down many of their outposts – Towednack, Zennor, Trencrom, Carfury among others – although the Countess of Huntingdon's Connection keeps its rare banner flying in St Ives.

How that latter-day saint, John Wesley, would have grieved over the backsliding: he who found 'some life, even at Zennor', and who, having been stoned by the 'rude, gaping, staring rabble-rout' of Newlyn, cried out 'Surely God will have a people even in this place where we have so long seemed only to beat the air.'

But it may be that the Holy Spirit, like the wind, blows too fiercely for dogma to endure in Penwith. I had better confess a prejudice: I am a Quaker, and although Friends, least of all, can hardly be said to have struck deep roots in the peninsula, I recall George Fox writing (in the year 1660): 'At Land's End there was an honest man, a fisherman, convinced, that became a faithful minister: of whom I told Friends he was like Peter.' Maybe not Peter the fisher of men, but Peter the rock; and perhaps the best thing any disciple can do in this land is to wait upon God like the rocks, in stillness and silence.

The Sea, The Sea . . .

If Penwith is a conversation between earth and sky, it is also
one between land and sea; though I have the impression that
Penwithians converse less intimately with the sea than they
used to. Maybe it was childhood fantasy, but surely, fifty
years ago, there were more little boats in the coves, and old
fishermen always happy to take you out for a few hours'
spinning for mackerel? Boats, tackle and fuel cost a lot more
now, it is true, and fresh fish has become something of an
embarrassment. Housewives, they say, don't care to handle it
any more; or, if they do, expect only cod, haddock or plaice;
that is, if they have advanced beyond frozen fillets and fish
fingers.

Mackerel is now sucked up by floating vacuum-cleaners
from Poland, rather than hauled in by hand-line. It is even
being smoked and served up as pub lunches at over a pound a
head. If you want to be a successful fisherman today you have
to use a bigger boat, more expensive equipment, have capital
behind you, and keep nagging the government for protection
against foreigners and up-country men. Look into Newlyn or
St Ives harbours and you will find that Cornishmen do
manage to make a living like that. They land the best crab in
the world and lobsters so huge that only London and Paris
restaurants can afford them. But there are not many of the
old-timers left in the coves, spreading their risks by doing a
bit of fishing, a bit of farming and maybe a bit of mining as
well. All around the coast there are places where there used to
be a few boats, hauled up in the winter, but where now there
are none at all.

Still the conversation continues between the rocks and the
waves. You can spend hours contemplating the battle and

letting it wash through your mind – either on the grand scale of the bays at Gurnard's Head or the Logan Rock, or in miniature wherever the waves sluice between a pair of rocks or surge and foam into a chasm. Part of the art of looking at Penwith is to find such miniature landscapes *within* the landscape, the boulder that is a mountain, the pool that is a lake.

The effect, I find, is something like meditation. The rustling of the sea against the cliffs resembles that continuous 'white sound' that some dentists use to kill pain. It anaesthetizes the worrying intellect, so that you come away refreshed. And even though it can be deafeningly loud, making it hard to do any constructive reasoning, you may find that your unconscious mind has born fruit.

There is a huge restlessness about the sea. How then can it be soothing? Because, I think, it confronts you with that hackneyed truth, easy to forget in cities, of the insignificance of man against nature. The streams about Penwith are water that is young and feminine. But the sea is old and male. It keeps on and on, battering at the cliffs. The cliffs stand unmoved, hurling it back. And yet you know – you can see – that the waves will win in the end, and that one day that headland will collapse and that Land's End is inching its way closer to London. One day, you feel, the sea will get *you*. There is a lot to be said for burial at sea:

> Me, dead, return to my infinity.
> Resolve my body, salt to salt.
> And let oblivion remember my bones once more,
> That were put forth like froth upon the shore.

Penwithians make fine lifeboat crews, but on the whole they are not the deep-sea-goers that Falmouth or Saltash men are. Inshore fishing, crab-and-lobstering and, formerly, seining, is more in their line. They used to indulge in a little short-range piracy, and like everyone else in Cornwall they smuggled until, during the 1830s, the revenue men got too successful. But Penwith coasts are tricky even in the daylight, and the more lucrative markets for brandy and tobacco were further east, towards Falmouth. There you could hope to bring in a decent-sized lugger or cutter, and the kind of scenes described by Daphne du Maurier really did take place, with kegs and hogsheads and pistols in the moonlight.

The Land's End got more than its fair share of the wrecking; provided you remember that actually luring vessels on to the rocks was not really part of the business – firstly because it would have been extremely difficult, and secondly because it was hardly necessary. The 'wracking' that shocked George Fox so deeply was the looting of ships that had already struck, often to the total neglect of any survivors, unless they happened to be wearing anything the Cornish fancied or were carrying something of value about their persons. In time of war, heavily laden troop transports often passed by Land's End and if one was wrecked, the casualties could be on much the same scale as the crash of a jumbo-jet today.

The people of Penwith had the knack of stripping a vessel down to her ribs within a few hours, outraging not just the humanitarian instincts of men like Fox, but the middle-class sense of private property. I should hate to cause offence, but judging from the tales of the bounty gleaned from the beaches during the two World Wars, and from what happened to a freezer-trawler that quite recently ran on to the rocks near Mousehole, traces of that knack have lingered on. The world's ship-owners have taken unconscious revenge on the peninsula by releasing hideous oil-slicks against it, the worst from the wreck of the *Torrey Canyon*.

Lest you should imagine that Penwith is still a dangerous place for shipwrecked mariners, let me recount what happened in Porthgwarra Cove (near Porthcurno) only a few years back. A Brazilian of Danish descent built himself a schooner out of reinforced concrete, and with only his wife and small child for company, bravely set sail out of Rio for Copenhagen. He navigated successfully from the South Atlantic into the North, turned right at the Bay of Biscay, and then became so exhausted that he fell asleep in the Western Approaches with the bows pointing at Penwith. To their horror, the inhabitants of Porthgwarra watched as the schooner, with all sails set, ran majestically on to their rocks in full daylight. The concrete cracked, the hull filled with water, and the Danish Brazilian and his family scrambled ashore to contemplate their total ruin.

Professional salvage attempts failed. But local ingenuity did not. Penwithians combed their countryside for the empty oildrums and plastic containers with which it is scattered, packed them into the hull at low water, and when the tide rose the schooner floated clear. Soon after, they towed it into Penzance and patched it with new cement. Fox would have been deeply touched, as indeed were the Brazilians. I wonder what legend this tale will have turned into, five hundred years from now.

Porthcurno is the last resting-place (though perhaps resting is hardly the word) of the demon Tregeagle. Next to the Mermaid of Zennor, his legend is probably the most famous and certainly the most imposing of all those in Penwith. Apart from the fact that it ends in perpetual motion, it would make a splendid opera, full of solo parts and choruses and graphic interludes. It is a fine example of an elemental myth devised to explain a natural phenomenon, being elaborated with local names and details and (surely) an injection of something that did really happen into a legend that is as old as Sisyphus.

Jan Tregeagle (sometimes 'Tergagle') was steward or bailiff to a considerable landowner over Bodmin way. According to one version, he was a real seventeenth-century person who lived at Trevorder, in the parish of St Breock, and his tombstone was still visible in the churchyard there 150 years ago. However, his is the sort of story that might have been posthumously attached to any oppressor of the poor. Worse than that, it is said Tregeagle had somehow been responsible for the deaths of his own sister, wife and children.

One day he was in the churchtown collecting the quarter's rents, and lining his own pocket. When one of the tenants paid up, Tregeagle pretended to mark a cross against his name but failed to touch pen to paper. Shortly after, Death called to him and Tregeagle, in terror, disgorged his wealth to the Church, begging the priests to save his soul from perdition.

Long they battled with the demons who had come to claim their rightful prey, but in the end powerful exorcisms succeeded and Tregeagle was laid in hallowed ground, temporarily at peace.

It did not last. The books were examined and the unjust steward's peculations discovered. There were fearful wranglings at law, and eventually the tenant whose rent had been pocketed was called before the court and asked why there was no receipt against his name. 'I paid Tregeagle,' he swore. 'But how can you prove that, with Tregeagle in his grave?' sneered the judge. 'Perhaps my chaplain will be so good as to summon his spirit to the witness box?'

The chaplain, a good man who was convinced of the tenant's innocence, bowed his head in agonized prayer. The windows darkened, the wind rose, suddenly the door crashed open and in strode the figure of Tregeagle, clasping his shroud about him. Those in the courtroom fled to the walls in horror and clung there, crossing themselves. But the judge on his bench sternly commanded the spectre to take the oath and then required of it: 'Jan Tregeagle, did you or did you not receive the rent offered by this tenant?' Tregeagle sighed a heavy sigh. 'Alas,' he replied, 'I did receive it, though I kept the money for myself and made no mark in my ledger.' 'You may go,' said the judge to the tenant. 'And now, Mister Chaplain, be so good as to return this witness to whence he came. It will be for some other power to punish him for the wrong he has done, and this court can no longer endure the stench of his corruption.'

In his best ecclesiastical Latin, the chaplain commanded Tregeagle to be gone. But outside the courthouse, the demons could be heard howling for him and the phantom would not budge. 'My lord,' said the chaplain gravely, 'the pity of God for an innocent man was able to bring him here, but Heaven now rejects him and nothing I can do will send him hence.'

Churchmen from far and wide were summoned to remove Tregeagle, and at last one was found holy enough. But a bargain had to be struck, for Tregeagle would not leave if it meant falling into the hands of Satan. So a contract was agreed under which his spirit was bound to Dozmary Pool, up on the moors, to bail it empty with a leaky limpet-shell – a task that would stretch into eternity since, as everyone knew, Dozmary Pool is bottomless.

And so Tregeagle bailed as Satan and his Hell hounds circled and snapped at his heels. Year after year the futile task went on, until at last, maddened by despair, Tregeagle flung the limpet-shell from him and raced off westwards with the hellish hunt in pursuit (indeed, you may hear them at it on many a stormy night). Almost they had him, but Tregeagle managed to drag himself to the hermit's cell on Roche Rock, where he dashed his head through the east window above the altar and laid claim to sanctuary even as the hounds tore at his back. It would be one of the high points of the opera: outside the yelling of the demons, inside the holy man intoning his prayers and Tregeagle's suspended head shouting blasphemies.

Eventually two more saints were found, powerful enough to lead him away and fetter him to another task, that of binding the sands of Padstow with ropes of sand. But his exasperated cries drove the citizens mad, and they secured St Petroc himself (never mind the seventeenth century any more) to remove Tregeagle to the south coast. His task now was to carry sacks of sand across the estuary of Loe River from Bereper to Porthleven, a task as futile as the one before since the currents kept sweeping it back again. The town of Helston, which was served by the river, was as much disturbed by enraged howls as ever Padstow had been. And when Tregeagle was tripped by a demon, depositing his sand across the mouth of the river and blocking it to this day, it was clear that once again Tregeagle had to go.

This time all the saints in Cornwall were gathered and it was agreed that Tregeagle must be given employment where there was nobody to disturb – or nobody that mattered. This clearly meant Penwith, and the final act of the opera shows Tregeagle engaged for evermore in sweeping the sand out of Porthcurno – surely the huge sandbar of Pednevounder, below the Logan Rock – either into Nanjizal, just short of Land's End or, according to some versions, clear round

Land's End into Whitesand Bay. There is no sign of the job being anywhere near completion, and if Tregeagle is still howling, Penwithians are inured to it by now. It may even be, I suppose, that he has settled down not too energetically to enjoy one of the pleasantest spots on the peninsula.

Tregeagle's activities explain not only a couple of annoying sandbars, but the comings and goings of the sand elsewhere. I know two or three small coves which may have a pleasant beach one year and nothing but pebbles the next. Tregeagle has been at work. One such place is Veor Cove, near Zennor, where at times the whole parish can play football – and at others you can hardly hobble across the rocks. How conditions were when the Zennor Mermaid was active, history does not relate.

What it does tell us is that there was once a young man called Matthew Trewhella who sang a brave tenor in the church choir there. One day, as the service began, a fine lady was seen to enter and took her seat apart from the congregation, just beside the door. Nobody knew who she was, but it was clear what had brought her there, for throughout the service she fixed young Matthew with a long and longing gaze. Her eyes, it is said, were green as seaweed; her tumbling hair as gold as the sand; and her dress shimmered like a shoal of pilchards breaking the water.

Back she came, Sunday after Sunday, until Matthew could not mistake her infatuation. But as the vicar rose to give the final blessing, she invariably slipped from her place, and was gone by the time the congregation reached the door.

One Sunday, Matthew determined to solve the mystery. During the last verse of the hymn he, too, slipped away and was in time to see the lady gliding down towards the sea. How we know what follows is hard to tell, unless somebody else was hard on their heels, but it is said the lady turned as if she was expecting Matthew, took him by the arm, and hurried him faster and faster along the stream. Along it? Did they even tumble into it, perhaps, to be washed away?

In any case, Matthew Trewhella was never seen again, or not in the lifetime of his parents. Years later, however, a passing ship put into the cove to draw water from the stream.

The watering party had gone ashore and the captain was on watch, when a voice was heard calling him from the sea: a woman's voice. 'Captain!' it cried. 'Will'ee haul up thine anchor? For 'tis blocking the door of my cave and I can't get in to my Matthy and our children.' Looking over the side, the captain saw a mermaid – well, let us say a young lady – with green eyes and golden hair. 'Did 'ee say Matthew?' he quavered. "ess, Matthy Trewhella,' said the lady impatiently. 'Now haul up thy hook!' And as the sailor jumped to it, she dived and was gone. If you doubt that there was a mermaid at Zennor, you may see her with a comb and a glass in her hand on an old pew-end in the church.

There are mermaids in other English churches (for example, in Norfolk), there as a warning to the faithful against the beauty which entices but deceives, though none of them has a story like Zennor's. Seals must be part of the explanation. They are far from uncommon along this coast and they do have a habit of coming up to stare at you. There are mermaid – and mer*man* – stories at Lamorna and round the Lizard peninsula, too. I should not put it past some young lady of Zennor to have teased a gullible sailor by playing the part of a mermaid and invoking the name of the vanished Matthy.

But there are two other considerations suggesting something real behind the fairy tale. The first is the name Trewhella or Trewhela, which is a genuine local name. The second follows the Alfred-and-the-cakes approach: why this particular story if there was not something in it? If there *was* a Matthew Trewhella whose voice was outstanding in a parish noted for its singing; if a woman from a ship trading round that coast admired him and kept making eyes at him; if they did elope together by sea, or at worst were drowned together; then might not the story have gone round – Oh, Matthy, he was taken away by a mermaid? His family might have encouraged the legend to cover their shame. Everybody believed in witchcraft; and by the time the Droll-tellers had embroidered it a bit, neighbouring parishes would have lapped it up. Meanwhile, Matthy was probably up in Padstow, happy with his green-eyed lady.

It was pilchards, rather than mermaids, that brought

Penwith and the sea closest together. They have not been on
such intimate terms since the great shoals left, whether from
caprice or from overfishing, towards the end of the last
century. For almost two centuries before that, pilchards had
been as regular a crop as oats or barley, arriving for harvest at
much the same time of year. In August and September they
appeared in enormous numbers off the far west of Cornwall,
one shoal in 1869 stretching for thirty miles. The catches were
prodigious and sound more like modern oil industry statis-
tics. In the 1860s, St Ives could man some 250 nets: at a single
draught one of them brought in 3,500 hogsheads or nearly 8
million fish – not the record, for in 1851 another had taken
5,600 hogsheads or 12 million fish. Even little Treen, in
Zennor, managed 600 hogsheads within a week.

A tiny fraction of the catch was eaten locally or sent off
fresh by train. The bulk of the pilchard catch was not even
destined for Britain, but for the continent. During the
Napoleonic Blockade, efforts were made to find an alternative outlet by shipping to the West Indies, for plantation
owners to feed to their slaves; but it was the Mediterranean
and especially the Italian market that really fancied the fish. In
1868, Naples took many thousand hogsheads, with Genoa,
the Adriatic and Leghorn close behind.

These, of course, were salt pilchards, and the process of
curing them was almost as important as that of catching them
and occupied large premises and hundreds of women and
girls. As soon as the fish were brought to land, they were
heaved out of the boats with large wooden shovels into
wheelbarrows or carts and trundled into the salting house.
Here the stone floor had been scrubbed clean and the women
were waiting for them, each with a bucket of salt. First a thin
layer of salt was spread on the floor, then a layer of pilchards,
then a layer of salt, then a layer of pilchards facing the other
way, and so on until a stack about four feet high had been
made with nothing but alternate noses or tails peeping out.
Here the pilchards remained for five or six weeks, oozing
unpleasantly and 'crying for more', as the saying went, while
their air-sacs popped and wheezed. The oil that seeped out
was clarified and sold, and when the process was complete the

fish were unstacked, washed in salt water, and packed up in barrels for export. The prices fetched were seldom high, and in the early part of the nineteenth century the business groaned under the imposition of a government salt tax.

But it was the catching of the pilchard that caused the real excitement. Every harbour that engaged in it would have one or more huers' cottages on the cliffs, manned by observers whose job it was not only to raise the hue-and-cry (traditionally 'Hevva! Hevva!') when a shoal was sighted, but also to direct operations like an orchestral conductor. For this they used a furze, or gorse, bush – waving it to right or left according to the movement of the shoal, pumping it up and down, or circling it over their heads.

The seine, a continuous curtain of net about a thousand feet long by sixty or seventy feet deep, had leads along the bottom edge and corks along the top. The initial object was to row round the shoal, shooting the net and encircling the fish. This was done from a large, sturdy boat that took a considerable effort to row, and it was accompanied by at least one smaller boat and a fleet of others to carry off the catch. Encirclement of the shoal called for close attention to the huers' signals, and sometimes the fish would panic and break away. But when it was successful a second boat would enter the rink, scare the fish into the centre by thrashing the water, and then lower under the shoal what was known as the tucking net, in which the pilchards were then drawn to the surface. Now was the moment when everything exploded – the sea, the shoal, the caution of the men. Pilchards were hauled out by their thousands in baskets, men worked knee-deep in fish, anything that would float was laden to the gunnel. Just twice in my life I have experienced something like it: once, in Ceylon, when I was snorkelling near Galle and was actually seined with a shoal of mackerel by Singhalese fishermen (what panic! what dashing hither and thither within the net!), and the second time, in the 1930s, when I witnessed the seining of a shoal onto a beach in the Isles of Scilly. Whether they were pilchards or not I cannot remember – the last great shoals of St Ives were just before the First World War – but I shall never forget the feeling of riches, of profligate quantity. And so it was. We shall not look upon its like again.

They are wondering now whether there is oil of another kind to be got from the sea off Penwith – not in it, but under it. If North Sea oil, why not Celtic Sea oil? The geologists are dubious, but some drilling has been done out there, south of Ireland, and men have been seen prowling the Hayle estuary, allegedly summing up its potential as a base for rig support ships. At least one local estate agent has been heard pondering the effect on Penwith property values. Another theory has it that vast flexible rafts will be moored off Land's End, generating electricity with the massive rise and fall of the waves; but it would have to be a very tough flexible raft that survived a week or two of that sea at its worst.

For it certainly is a cruel sea, one to be treated with great respect. Its teeth have made Penwith what it is, and one day, if it fancies, it will bite Penwith right off.

Little People

With great delight, Robert Hunt records as just told to him an account of what would surely have been the last capture of a fairy in England. It so happens that the story appears in Bottrell's collection, too, with variations, so that I doubt if the news was quite as hot as Hunt pretended. Be that as it may, they are in general agreement as to what happened:

A man was cutting furze on the slopes of the long hill between Trendrine and Zennor. (Inevitably, one must pass the spot somewhere on the B3306.) At about mid-day he was looking for a comfortable spot to eat his lunch, when he found, on a bank of 'griglans' or heather, a little creature 'no bigger than a cat' and fast asleep. Bottrell dresses it up in a green coat, sky-blue breeches, diamond-buckled shoes and a three-cornered hat; but Hunt gives no details of its costume. Both agree that the furze-cutter picked the creature up and slipped it into the protective cuff he was wearing on one arm and took it home. There it was tipped out on to the hearth, to the delight of the children.

The fairy child seemed happy enough to play with the family who named him Bobby Griglans and fed him on milk and blackberries. Bobby would sit on the wood-stack and sing like a robin, or dance for hours to the clicking of the goodwife's knitting needles. But they were all determined not to let him go free until he had told them where the crocks of gold were hidden upon the hill.

One day the furze-cutter heard the neighbours coming up the track to his cottage, and anxious that they should not share his secret, shut the fairy up in the barn along with the children. After a while, the children became bored and took Bobby out with them to play hide-and-seek round the furze-rick. There, to their amazement they found a tiny man and woman – little bigger than Bobby – peeping and peering into the rick and calling 'O my tender Skillywidden! Where can'st'a be?' 'Go back now,' said the little fellow to the children, 'for 'tis my mammy and my daddy come for me,' and he darted into the arms of his fairy mother who scurried him off into the bushes, never to be seen again. Both Hunt and Bottrell agree that the children received a sound thrashing for letting Skillywidden escape with the crocks undiscovered.

Wrote Henry Quick of Zennor:

> *The Cornish drolls are dead, each one;*
> *The fairies from their haunts have gone;*
> *There's scarce a witch in all the land,*
> *The world has grown so learn'd and grand.*

And there is no doubt in my mind that it was the advance of schooling and up-country sophistication that shamed the fairies out of Penwith. Not that they were ever called 'fairies' in their heyday, but piskies, spriggans, or 'small people'. Down the mines they were called knockers or buccas, and a buggaboo was originally a *bucca-dhu* or black spirit.

Hunt tells us there were several distinct varieties of fairy folk: the Small People proper, who were the gradually dwindling spirits of the first inhabitants of Cornwall – possibly of the Druids – who could not go to Heaven since they were unbaptized, yet were too innocent to be condemned to Hell. And so they lingered on, getting smaller and smaller, until finally they would turn into ants. Then there were the Spriggans, whom some thought to be the ghosts of the giants, since they guarded the hill-forts, quoits and barrows and were responsible for sundry disasters such as barns collapsing and cattle vanishing. After them came the Piskies or Pigseys, Puck-like creatures whose activities, though annoying, were a good deal less dreadful and more in the nature of practical jokes. Leading travellers astray at night was a speciality, best countered by turning one's coat inside out.

The mine Buccas, while given to similar pranks in their

own world, were rather more than an underground variety of Piskey, for they came of a totally different racial stock. Every miner knew that Buccas were the spirits of ancient Jews, sent by the Romans to work as slaves in the tin mines, and that if there was one thing to be avoided at all costs it was infuriating them by making the sign of the cross. Their distant knocking and chatter could be heard in abandoned workings, and it was prudent to leave a few crumbs of pasty or heavy-cake for them at the end of one's lunch break. The old tradition insisted upon a link between the ancient tin-trade and the Jews: Hunt was once assured that St Paul had come to Cornwall to buy tin, and had preached the gospel there – which was probably a confusion with the Breton St Pol, to whom Paul Church is dedicated. The real Jewish connection is almost certainly much later, with mediaeval Jewish tin-dealers who had long lost any connection with the Holy Land.

Finally in this fairy catalogue came the Browneys, who were benevolent household spirits, also to be appeased by the leaving of food and drink before the hearth. And if the offerings were gone in the morning, who could be sure that it was only the mice that had taken them?

Such hierarchies are probably to be found all over Europe and far beyond. To some degree they are nature spirits, accounting for the special personalities that surround every well-known natural feature, every hill, stream, cave or forest. In another way they are the explanation of why things inexplicably go wrong, why a man loses his way on a moor he has crossed dozens of times before, why the cattle stray from their normal grazing, why the sheep fall over the cliff-edge, why the milk turns sour, why a perfectly sound piece of mine-working suddenly collapses. But there are certain special features of the Cornish elf-kingdom.

It seems to me that the notion of the Small People as the faint remnants of the original pre-Celtic inhabitants must enshrine a memory that they really *were* a smaller race that was gradually squeezed away into remote corners, getting fewer and fewer, less and less human in the eyes of those who were replacing them. As for the Spriggans and their pots of gold, those who occupied the hill-forts very probably did conceal valuables in crocks that were unearthed from time to time. We know that some of the ancient graves yielded cremation urns and very occasionally golden ornaments.

An interesting point about Skilly*widden* is that on the other side of Trendrine Hill, not far from Towednack church, is a tiny farm by the name of Skilly*wadden*. Its Cornish meaning I have not been able to penetrate, but local enquiry once produced a vague memory that 'it was the name of a fairy'.

There was a strong tradition in Penwith and elsewhere of the Changeling Child – so strong that as late as 1843 a Penzance man was prosecuted for 'shamefully ill-using' a three-year-old boy whom he believed to be a fairy substitute for his real son. The child was frequently kicked, beaten, kept without food, and when only fifteen months old (it was said) left out in a tree on a cold Christmas Day. That was precisely the treatment tradition prescribed for forcing the Spriggans to return the real child. What the Spriggans should have done then was to answer the cries of their own offspring, fetch it down out of the tree and leave the human infant in its place. Incidentally, the Penzance man was acquitted on the grounds that there was no evidence to connect him, rather than his servants, with the cruel treatment. He was, however, hooted out of town.

To say that a sickly or ill-favoured child was a changeling would have been one way of saving face and denying responsibility for it. But there was another factor which may help to explain the persistence of a half-belief in fairies. The Cornish have never been less inclined towards the pleasures of the flesh than anyone else, and the Church in Cornwall was no more tolerant of them. Bastardy was a great disgrace (remember the suicide at Morvah) and many a girl must have borne or aborted her child on the moors and left it there, perhaps to perish, perhaps to be rescued by some passer-by. I suspect that some at least of the tiny figures seen or heard among the furze bushes may have been only too human. They were, indeed, 'small people', and the tradition that the moors were haunted by the spirits of the unbaptized thus assumes a bitter truth.

Hunt credits Wesleyanism with stamping out the old ignorance which attributed sickliness in children to the intervention of the Spriggans. But there are hints, here and there, that abduction by the fairies was occasionally used to cover up a well-intentioned practical joke. There is, for example, the tale of Betty Stogs of Morvah, a slut who was married to an equally unattractive husband known as Jan the Mounster. The two of them were permanently drunk on gin, and their unfortunate baby was ill-fed, filthy and frequently left alone. This could prove disastrous in the old Cornish cottages, where crawling children all too easily fell in the open hearth or – worse still – could be devoured alive by marauding pigs. The neglect of Betty's child evidently proved more than somebody could bear, for one day Betty rolled home to find the cradle empty and the child nowhere to be seen.

It was dawn before the cat came mewing into the cottage and insisted on being followed outside. It led the way to a clump of gorse, where – lo and behold! – the baby lay sleeping on a tuffet of moss, its skin washed and pink, its clothes freshly laundered, and a bunch of sweet violets in its hand. Everyone concluded that the Small People (not the Spriggans, notice) had taken pity on the child and decided to teach the Mounster and his slovenly wife a lesson at the same time. Evidently it worked, for from then onwards Betty became a sober and diligent mother, and no more conscientious father than Jan was to be found in all Morvah.

The trouble with fairies is that they are (except on special occasions) invisible, which must have been their ultimate downfall when the day of scientific Show Me arrived. Very few people claimed to have had such direct experience as the captors of Skillywidden, and about the best evidence anyone could cite was the persistent behaviour of animals in a manner that could only be explained by the existence of the small folk. For no good reason a cow would start holding back half her milk – for the small folk; or a horse would be found in the morning ridden to exhaustion – by the small folk. Cocks would be found deprived of their stylish tail-feathers – stolen for the small folk's caps. And the tufts of sheep's wool found on the blackthorn bushes had surely been left there by tiny spinners. Carrying this further, there was no doubt that the clumps of sea-pinks growing inaccessibly on the cliffs were planted there as fairy gardens, and that sudden eruptions of thistles in the fields were the attempts of fairies to keep humans off their dancing grounds.

Or so we are told by the Victorian collectors, though I wonder, myself, whether some of these are not too sentimental for the native Cornish. They sound to me as if they were designed to please children rather than to express the deeper mysteries of the adult world. There is an area, however, in which the world of faery and the world of spells and magic overlap and we find ourselves in the mysteriously significant, real-unreal world of the so-called Fairy Tale. Such tales appeal on more than one level to the folk-memory, to the psychological instincts of family relationships, to the sense of wonder and horror, and to our taste for simple story-telling forms. As usual, the Droll-tellers saw to it that they were spiced with plenty of local details that would bring them literally home to the hamlets of Penwith; and I know of none more interesting in this way than the tale of Cherry of Zennor. For while it has at least one classic fairy tale embedded in it, there is a lot more that has the ring of fact.

According to Hunt, Cherry was one of the ten children of Old Honey, who lived in a two-roomed cottage with a 'talfat', or sleeping-gallery, on the cliffside at Treen, close by the Gurnard's Head. They were poor, living mostly on limpets, fish and potatoes, but they were healthy, good-looking and respectable.

Cherry, however, longed for a new dress so that she could take the world by storm next Morvah Fair. There she was, sixteen years of age, and without hope of the simplest finery for the occasion. And since Zennor held out little hope of enrichment, she determined to find domestic service in the lush country on the south side of the peninsula. Tying up a few possessions in a bundle, she took the road towards Ludgvan and Gulval and set out to make her modest fortune.

When she reached the Lady Downs and the rooftops of Treen were no longer to be seen, the heart almost went out of her. She sank down 'on a stone by the four cross roads' and wept. When she looked up, a fine gentleman stood before her, having appeared, it seemed, from nowhere. He enquired the way to Towednack and then asked gently if anything was the matter? Cherry explained that she had set out to look for service but was now of more than half a mind to run home again. 'Do not do that,' exclaimed the gentleman, 'for this luck must be meant for the two of us! I had set out myself to find just such a girl as you, and here you are!' Then he told Cherry that he had recently been left a widower and needed someone to take charge of his little son. He lived, he said, down in the low countries and if she would come with him, Cherry could start work that very day.

She agreed, and taking her by the hand the gentleman led her downhill, through lanes so shaded with trees that the sun hardly shone through, past hedges of honeysuckle and boughs laden with apples, until they came to a crystal stream running across the lane. There was no bridge and Cherry wondered how they were to cross: but the gentleman slipped his arm about her waist and whirled her over like a partner in a dance. The lane got darker and narrower and fell rapidly downhill. At length it brought them to a gate, which opened into a garden the like of which Cherry had never seen, so rich was it with fruits and flowers, so clamorous with birdsong, so sweet with drifting perfumes. And running down the garden path, crying out with joy to see his Papa, came her new charge – the little boy. He was, perhaps, three years of age; but with a strange look of experience about him, his eyes were so bright and penetrating, even crafty (thought Cherry).

After the boy, there came stumbling and grumbling the most hideous old hag, who dragged him, scolding, back into the house, and who shot Cherry a glance that went through her heart like a gimlet. That, explained the gentleman, apologetically, was his late wife's grandmother; but Cherry need not fear her, for as soon as Cherry could cope on her own, the old lady would go, and high time too that she did.

Despite her ill humour, Aunt Prudence (as she was called) had prepared an appetizing dinner for Cherry and then led her to the nursery where she was to sleep with her little boy. Her instructions were strict: she was not to speak to the child all night, and was to keep her eyes tightly shut, whether she was asleep or no, or she might see things she had no business seeing. At daybreak she was to rise, take the boy to a spring in the garden, wash him in it and anoint his eyes with salve from a crystal box which she would find in a cleft of rock. On no account (said Aunt Prudence with terrible emphasis) was she to touch the ointment to her own eyes, or it would be the end of all happiness for her. No: she must replace the box in its hiding place, and call for the cow. This would come with no further effort, and when Cherry had milked a full bucket from it, she was to draw off a bowl for the boy's breakfast and bring him home.

All of which Cherry did faithfully. She bathed the child, anointed his eyes, left him to play happily by himself among the flowers, and then had only to call softly: 'Pruit! Pruit! Pruit!' for a fair and gentle milch cow to appear from among the trees and stand waiting to be milked. It gave exactly the right quantity, and always held back the sweetest milk till the last.

During the day, Cherry's duties were far from light. She scoured the pans and dishes, scalded the milk, made the butter, and when all was accomplished in the kitchen, must set to work weeding and picking in the garden. But Zennor girls are sturdy and hard-working, and Cherry's new master was delighted with her, rewarding her with a kiss for every task completed. This made her still less of a favourite with the old grandmother. She had always forbidden Cherry to enter any other room in the house but the nursery and the kitchen; but one day, taking a ring of keys from about her waist, she conducted Cherry to an apartment that made her gasp. Its floor seemed made of glass, and standing around the walls – some on shelves, others upon the floor – were people who had been turned to stone, some of them entire, others with only their head and shoulders left. Cherry was appalled, certain now that she was in the palace of an enchanter, but Aunt Prudence told her to stop her whimpering and set her to work polishing what appeared to be 'a coffin upon six legs'. When Cherry peered fearfully over her shoulder the old woman stamped her foot and cried: 'Harder! Harder! Faster!

Faster!', until Cherry rubbed so hard that the box shifted and gave out a melancholy groaning sound, as if the body within was coming to life. Cherry screamed and fainted; her master hurried in, and though he revived her tenderly, he threw Aunt Prudence out of the house for violating his strictest instructions that the girl should never be allowed in his secret apartments.

'Now we are alone together, Cherry my dear,' said the fine gentleman. But in truth, it was she that was alone; for the master went riding off at dawn, as if going hunting, and in the evening, after supper, withdrew to the secret apartments, whence followed the sound of music and laughter. Cherry was happy enough with her lot, and yet, at the same time, wistfully unhappy at the thought of happiness denied her.

One day at the spring a wicked thought crept into her head. If the master would not let her into his secrets, she would withhold one from him: while there was nobody watching, she would try just a crumb of the forbidden ointment. At the merest touch of it her eye began to burn as if a spark of furze had blown into it from the hearth. In a frenzy, she plunged her face into the pool beside the spring, blinking her eyelid to wash out the burning salve. As the pain eased, she stared through the shimmering water and saw, afar off, a host of tiny people leaping and frolicking among the rocks. Yet they were *not* afar off: they were under her very nose, at the bottom of the pool – but they were tiny, as tiny as the very pebbles amongst which they played hide-and-seek, and yet they were perfect in every naked detail. Staring more closely, Cherry was amazed to see – conducting the revels – none other than her fine master himself.

Slowly she raised her head and looked about her. The whole garden was now swarming with the Little People, snoozing in the flowers, swinging on twigs of blossom, leap-frogging over fallen apples and teasing the bumble-bees with blades of grass. And as she looked to where the child, her charge, had wandered, she realized the reason for his happiness: the whole fairy rout was playing for his amuse-ment – only now she was seeing them as clearly as he had always done.

Cherry was so vexed at the deception practised upon her that she snatched up the child, squirming and protesting, hurried him into the house and bolted the door. And that evening, after her master had ridden home, supped, and withdrawn to his private side of the house, she waited until the music began and tiptoed through to unmask that side of his life as well. When she came to the room with the glass floor and the stone people, she knelt down and peered through the keyhole with the eye that had been anointed. Once again, a scene of revelry; once again, a host of beautiful ladies; only now they were fully human in size, and richly dressed, and one of the ladies – robed like a queen – was drawing a jangly music from the coffin upon legs. Cherry could scarcely contain herself when she saw her master bend down and kiss the bare shoulders of the queen even more lovingly than he had kissed her own cheek.

Next morning he did not ride out, but stayed at home to pick the apple harvest. Cherry sulked and pouted, and when he began to humour her and slipped an arm about her waist, she slapped him and told him to jump in the spring and flirt with his own sort and leave a poor human girl alone. At once the birds ceased their singing, the sun clouded over, and so did her master's face. 'Cherry,' he demanded. 'Hast 'ee been using the salve from yon crystal box? I can see that 'tis so. And being so, I must banish 'ee from my home for ever and bring back Aunt Prudence. For I will account to nobody for my doings – I will have no spy about the place.' Nevertheless, the fairy master was merciful to Cherry, for he presented her with a bundle of new clothes almost too fine for Morvah Fair, and taking a lantern in his hand he led her back up the dark lanes till they came to the high ground once more. And there, as day broke, he left her on the Lady Downs where they had first met, promising her that if she was a good girl he would meet her again some day. Then he vanished.

When Cherry wandered back to the cottage on the cliffs, Old Honey crossed himself, believing her to be her own ghost. At first no-one would believe her story, but (says Hunt) she never varied it and, in the end, they all took it for the truth. Though she was never quite right in the head, thereafter, and on moonlit nights would stray over the Lady Downs, searching for her fairy master.

Easy enough to pick out the classic elements of fairy tale: Hunt also gives us the tale of Jenny Permuen of Towednack, who is engaged at 'the four cross roads on the Lady Downs' to take care of a fairy widower's child. No ointment is involved in this adventure, but it is in at least two other stories, in which it enables the human eavesdropper to spy the fairy doing some invisible shoplifting in Penzance Market. In the background of Cherry's tale there is also an echo of the primal myth of innocence lost in the Garden of Eden.

But that is not to say that young girls don't lose their innocence with great regularity, or that there may not have been a real Cherry of Zennor whose experience only went to show how sound the old legends were. Is it so improbable that such a girl *was* picked up by a fine gentleman, who indeed 'gave her a baby', sacked the interfering housekeeper, and kept his peasant plaything in the kitchen while entertaining the local gentry in his ballroom with its statuary and its spinet? Certainly not improbable that eventually he would tire of the girl and throw her out with some cheap finery to keep her mouth shut. The child? Probably it died, to his relief, making it all the easier to get rid of her. And when the girl came home, maybe ill and unhinged, her family may gratefully have seized upon the more fantastic parts of her tale as a cover-up to the murky truth: after all, didn't they fall in line with one or two legends that had always been current? Didn't it all show that such things do happen, far away on the other side of the Lady Downs?

Never mind the magic ointment part of it, although wizards and alchemists were always experimenting with formulae to bestow supernatural vision. Suppose we take the backbone of Cherry's tale seriously and see what there is to support it. For a start, we can put ourselves on the Lady Downs and see, quite literally, where we go from there. One difficulty is that there is now no 'road' that leads to Ludgvan and Gulval, or for that matter to Towednack, up on the Downs. However, there are paths and tracks where a rider or walker might go and – between a small farm called Mill

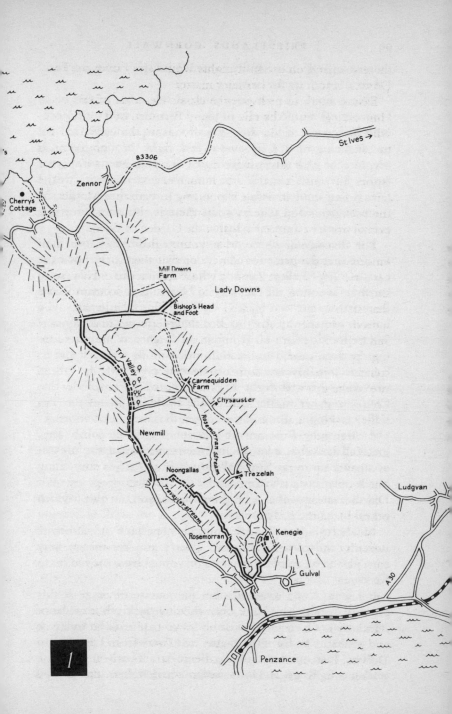

St Ives →

B3306

Zennor

Cherry's
Cottage

Mill Downs
Farm

Lady Downs

Bishop's Head
and Foot

Try Valley

Carnequidden
Farm

Chysauster

Rosemorran stream

Newmill

Noongallas

Trezelah

Ludgvan

Trevaylor stream

Rosemorran

Kenegie

Gulval

A30

1

Penzance

Downs and the delightfully named 'Bishop's Head and Foot'
– there are four tracks crossing.

Where next? The obvious thing at this point would be to
head almost immediately south, down the valley of Rosemorran Stream in the direction of Carnequidden Farm. We
might then go past Chysauster, fork right through Trezelah
and take the path towards Kenegie (which, as we shall see, is a
highly attractive target). The main thing wrong with this, I
feel, is that neither today nor at any historic time could the
route be described as densely overhung with trees. Nor is it
ever necessary to cross a stream.

The alternative, which presents some difficulties, too, is to
assume that the pair moved a little further west and took the
parallel Try Valley (also Trevaylor Stream). This soon
becomes wooded, all the way to Newmill and beyond, and
there are at least two places where the old track in the valley
bottom crosses the stream. But where are we really going?
We are looking for a large house with a garden, and there are
two perfect candidates within half a mile of each other,
Kenegie and Rosemorran, just where the two stream valleys
converge. At first sight one is tempted to conclude that
Cherry and her master must have come up out of the Try
Valley to Noongallas and then down the lane to Rosemorran.

At first sight, Rosemorran looks perfect for the job: a long,
thatched hall that even includes a room which the present
occupants know as 'the Ballroom'. But there is something
psychically unsatisfactory about it for our purposes. For
Rosemorran was once a religious house, and the ghost which
is said to haunt it is a monk – which is not at all in keeping
with Cherry's legend. I am, in fact, rather happy to eliminate
Rosemorran from the contest. Cherry and her master may
have passed by it, but somehow they must have moved on to
Kenegie.

If I seem to be glossing over the precise itinerary at this
point, it is because I have been holding back other evidence
which makes Kenegie irresistible. If you approach it today, it
will probably be from the B3311 on its way from Penzance to
St Ives, just outside Gulval. There is a board at the gate
announcing Kenegie Hotel and other delights, and as you

approach it along the drive that is what you will see – a disappointing late-Victorian building that has been lately mucked about with, and a clutter of holiday cabins with views of one another and not much else. But continue round to the back, to Kenegie Home Farm, and it begins to make sense: an old, haunted-looking building with a clock tower, and a pedigree going back at least to Tudor times. And I use the word 'haunted' deliberately. It is hard to say where the old house and the new overlap, but the official history of the Hotel (which is well worth acquiring) relates how it was haunted by the spirit of an elderly scolding housekeeper who could be heard arranging the furniture for company and screeching angrily: 'Quick! Come quick!' to which another voice would reply: 'Anon, anon!' Aunt Prudence, bullying Cherry? The Hotel history, anxious to reassure guests that they have nothing to worry about, insists that the ghostly housekeeper has long since been walled up in an oubliette and can, at worst, only be heard clicking her knitting needles.

As I shall record in the next chapter, Kenegie has been one of the most thoroughly haunted houses in the west, thanks largely to the Harris family that lived in one part of the house or another between about 1640 and 1775, and especially to one Wild Harris.

According to Bottrell, the old housekeeper was first employed by Wild Harris's father, and the younger man dismissed her upon the father's death. That seems to me near enough the tale of Cherry; and still more significant is the tradition that Wild Harris used to roam the moors and once abducted a local girl and kept her prisoner in the summerhouse which is still standing at one end of Kenegie's lawn. Wild Harris was also noted for his extravagant entertaining, and but for the fact that no child is attributed to him he fits the description of Cherry's fine gentleman very well. We have not, in fact, heard the last of him in this book.

Myself, I have never seen a ghost – even in Penwith – and I do not expect to. I cannot say I believe in spirits, though others may be more sensitive and are welcome to. What I do believe in is the reality of Cherry Zennor; indeed, I have a possible home for her, for on the cliffside near the Gurnard's

Head there is a ruined cottage with a gnarled ash tree growing out of it, contorted by the Atlantic gales. Even if Cherry is not exact, then she is at least the folk-type of many an innocent serving girl, taken advantage of by her master. Zennor, Morvah and Towednack – the High Countries – were too poor to produce any grander figures than the parish priest, and a girl who came to a place like Kenegie might have been forgiven for being carried away and feeling that she was living in a fairy tale.

But fairy tales, as the Brothers Grimm knew them, are often sordid and brutal: the Sleeping Beauty was awakened not by a kiss but by an act of rape. The Little People, the Spriggans and Buccas, have been toned down as bedtime stories for children; but as we shall now see, their elders kept alive the consciousness of a ghostly world of calculated evil.

Bumps in the Night

The Devil, it is said, never entered Cornwall. Arriving at the banks of the Tamar (like every other invader, he came from the East) he peered across and with alarm noted the Cornish diet: Ram Pie and Muggety Pie, Taddago Pie and Nattlin Pie, Conger Pie and Giblet Pie, Lammy Pie and Piggy Pie, Leeky, Tatey and Herby Pie, and Starry-Gazy Pie with the heads of the embedded pilchards peeping out through the crust. What if they should fancy a dish of Devilly Pie? Satan shuddered and contented himself with Devon.

Alas! I fear that all the saints in Penwith could not keep the Prince of Evil out. If you go up Carne Road, opposite the Newlyn Art Gallery, and keep along the path that meets it at the top and then left down a small neglected track, you will arrive at a large boulder overlooking the port, and you will notice that it bears a netlike pattern and is split in two. This is the Devil's work, and Bottrell relates it with a precise date (1592) and names.

The Devil, he says, had a mind to go fishing and stole himself a load of nets. Off he went, pursued by the members of Paul Church choir – Shepherd Pentreath, Jacky Kelynack, Benny Downing, Dick Keigwin and others – all determinedly chanting the Lord's Prayer and the Apostles' Creed at him. In a rage to escape them, the Devil leapt on to Tolcarn Rock, where the weight of him split the crag, tripping him up and forcing him to drop the nets. But before vanishing in the usual clap of thunder, he turned and cursed his pursuers with the promise that they would be smitten by a foreign power – which they duly were three years later when the Spaniards landed.

My own reaction to the tales of evil in Penwith is as divided as the rock. There is much in the landscape that is primitive, mysterious and pre-Christian; and yet, personally, I find it perfectly benign, perhaps because I approach it with affection and respect and get back from it what I put into it. From time to time I do experience one of those timeless moments that 'flash upon the inward eye'; but I have never felt any tingle of dread creep up the back of my neck, or shuddered as I passed over the moors at midnight. But the fact remains that the legends that would account for such dread often seem rooted in a later age than the tales of the giants, saints and fairies, as if folk believed in them longer.

Some years ago, a friend of mine was acting as chairman at a gathering of Cornish clergy which was being addressed by a psychiatrist. When the question period arrived, the visitor was asked how he would deal with cases of witchcraft. His response was mildly mocking, and soon a rumble of disapproval could be heard spreading round the hall. My friend felt a twitch at his sleeve, and turned to hear one of the platform party whisper to him 'Get him out of this quickly – we take these things seriously down here!' And indeed they do, in a discreet way. There is one parish in Penwith which is still believed to have its – highly respectable – coven of witches. There have been bizarre nocturnal goings-on in some of the remoter churches. And several years ago, a pentagram and a crucified seagull appeared in a ruined barn. The likelihood is that most such episodes are perpetrated by outsiders, by amateur dabblers in black magic who conduct their rituals with an open copy of Idries Shah in one hand, encouraged by the knowledge that the Satanist Aleister Crowley found the area stimulating. In one house where he is reputed to have stayed, two women were found, years later – one dead, the other raving that the Devil had shown himself. More recently I recall a local charmer who was stirring up a potion on her gas stove, when her television aerial was struck by lightning, blowing out the screen. The good lady confided to her acquaintances that she must have said the spell backwards: she had been trying to push power *out*, and instead it had been sucked *in*.

Witchcraft was certainly believed in while Bottrell and

Hunt were at work, and not merely preserved in the legends of days gone by. There was James Thomas (alias 'Jimmy the Wizard') of Illogan, who died in 1874 after many years lucrative practice in Penwith. His speciality was the protection against ill-wishing of ships sailing out of Hayle, which he achieved by the unnatural expedient of going to bed with the captain. The method was considered effective against almost any form of curse, and Jimmy spent an entire weekend with one young man he fancied, on the grounds that there were two spells on him requiring one night's attentions each. The *West Briton* considered him 'a drunken, disgraceful, beastly fellow, and ought to be sent to the treadmill'. Not much better was William Rapson Oates, a herbalist of Ludgvan, who was constantly being sent to jail for pretending to exorcize sorcery and who claimed to be regularly engaged by farmers in Devon and Cornwall, either to cure their cattle or to prevent ill-wishing.

How did one become a witch? The simplest method was to touch a Logan stone nine times at midnight – though some authorities insist this was not enough, that you had to climb on and off the stone nine times without rocking it. The strength of this tradition is demonstrated by the fact that witches and Logan stones have declined together – some of the stones simply carted off for building, others deliberately overthrown by the Church. There was one near Penzance, known as Maen-Amber or Mincamber, said to have been dedicated by Merlin with the prophecy that it should stand until England had a king no more: and, sure enough, when Cromwell came one of his lieutenants called Shrubsall overthrew the stone. Almost certainly he did this to destroy the pagan rites connected with it, and I began to wonder whether Lieutenant Goldsmith's overthrow of the Logan Rock at Treen may not have had more significance than he realized. St Levan, like Zennor, was a notable hotbed of witchcraft, but the sisterhood went into decline in both parishes when the rocks were interfered with.

There are some who believe that there never really were any witches – that it was all a figment of seventeenth-century Church hysteria. Certainly the allegations of flying on broomsticks (or stems of ragwort), of consorting with familiar imps and conjuring up storms were far-fetched. But, quite apart from the historic evidence to be found in the columns of old newspapers, there is one very good reason why some old women should have believed them-selves to be witches – and that is, that they believed other old women were, who had to be countered. How far their spells were effective is probably a matter of suggestion or psychological warfare. And since there is no reason to suppose that witchcraft was suddenly invented in historic times, there is every reason to believe that what they did was derived from pre-Christian practices, however garbled and distorted. I believe that there really were dances in the stone circles (and occasionally still are), and that the witches did sometimes gather on Midsummer's Eve with the local wizard and celebrate a fertility orgy. Wizards were always hereditary.

The Devil, his witches and one of the classic European fairy tales all come together without too much horror in the St Buryan legend of Duffy and the Devil. There is no suggestion here of any originality in the basic plot: it is Rumpelstiltskin, or (in Scotland) Whuppety-Stoorie, all over again. But it is the detail which is informative.

Duffy, an idle but good-looking slut, was engaged by Squire Lovel of Trove to spin his wool and knit stockings for him. Though she boasted she made the finest in the parish, the fact was that she had no idea of how to do either. Confronted with a loft-full of fleece, she stamped her pretty foot and cried out 'May the Devil do it, for all I care!' There was a stirring in the shadows, and out stepped a little man in black who bowed low to Duffy and assured her it would be his pleasure.

There was, however, the inevitable condition: 'I shall spin and knit for you for three full years; but after that, you must be mine – *unless* you can find out my name.' Three years seemed long enough to Duffy to guess any name under the sun, and so she agreed. The queer little man in black told her that whatever she wished for would be found complete 'under the black ram's fleece'.

And so it was: Duffy kept the Devil busy turning out all kinds of fine clothing which she claimed as her own work, but especially the stockings which the Squire wore on his constant hunting expeditions. Not furze nor thorn nor bramble, not stream nor swamp nor pool could scratch his legs or damp his bones. The only curious thing about this fantastic hosiery was that, to those who examined them carefully, there was always a single stitch dropped.

Duffy herself had done nothing whatever to earn the reputation she now enjoyed, but with all the time in the world for gadding about, she soon became sought after by half the likely lads in Penwith. Alarmed at the prospect of losing her, Squire Lovel married her himself and made her Lady Lovel (though her companions referred to her as Duffy Lady). Her new luxury went to her head, and Duffy was careless of the passing time until she suddenly realized that the three years were almost at an end. Now she haunted the wool-loft day after day, with lists of names in her hand. One after another she read them out, but the little man in black, crouched over the spinning wheel, denied every one of them, and began to eye her with an anticipation that made her flesh creep.

At last the time had run out, and on the morrow Duffy must surrender herself to her creditor. Came midnight, and she was seated miserably in her parlour trying to think of that one name which had so far escaped her, when the Squire burst in wild-eyed from his hunting. 'Duffy my dear,' he cried, 'you'll never guess what I have seen this night!' 'Nor will you guess where I must go tomorrow,' she groaned. Squire Lovel brushed that aside: 'I was hunting up near Dawns Men,' he gabbled, 'when the dogs started the finest hare you ever did see. She ran down the hill, past the Piper stones, and straight into the Fugoe Hole in Lamorna Bottoms. We went in after her – out flew all the owls and bats – and on and on we chased, for a mile or more. Then, round a corner, there were all the St Levan witches gathered round their fire in a great cavern. In the midst of them all, twirling his long forked tail, was a queer little fellow in black. Then the witches began to dance and sing:

> *Here's to the Devil*
> *With his wooden pick and shovel,*
> *Digging tin by the bushel*
> *With his tail cocked up!*

'And as they danced, the fellow in black was spinning round and round in the middle, laughing like a magpie. After a while, the witches all ran out of breath and sank to the ground: when the little fellow began leaping through the fire, hurling himself among the witches and kicking them soundly. And when he had done, he roared with laughter and sang out some words that you'll never guess, Duffy, though they were meant for *you!*'

At this, Duffy turned pale: 'For I?' 'That they were. Let me remember, now. Yes, he sang:

> '*O Duffy, my Lady, you'll never know what,*
> *But my name is . . .*' and the Squire paused, thoughtfully.

'What was it? What was it?' screamed Duffy in a frenzy, clinging to the Squire's coat and shaking him like a naughty child. 'What was his name, then?' 'Why, bless me, Duffy, if your shrieking hasn't driven it quite out of my head! Let me try again . . .' And the Squire bellowed:

> '*O Duffy, my Lady, you'll never know what,*
> *But my name is Terrytop, Terrytop, Top.*'

And at that, Duffy fell to the floor, sobbing and gasping:

> '*Terrytop, Terrytop, Terrytop, Top!*'

Next morning she was in the loft early. She wished until the pile of finery had pushed the ram's fleece up to the very roof, and every chest and press in the house was full to bursting.

Now the queer fellow in black was bowing low before her, with an unpleasantly obsequious leer, and reaching out to take her by the arm. 'Come, then, Duffy Lady,' he sneered.

'No more wasting time. A lady should never keep a gentleman waiting.'

'But a gentleman', said Duffy, flirtatiously, 'might give a lady her last chance or two.' 'You may have three,' snapped the Devil, 'but hurry up with it. My fault is, I'm too tender-hearted.' 'Then is your name Lucifer?' suggested Duffy. 'Pshaw! That riff-raff! Nothing like it!' 'Could you be Beelzebub?' 'I most certainly could not – though I believe he is a distant relative. That's the closest you've got and the closest you ever will. It's hardly worth trying any more.' And the Devil forgot his umbrage at being addressed as an inferior demon, and began to prance round Duffy pinching the most desirable portions of her anatomy.

'Then hands off – TERRYTOP!'

There was an enormous silence as the Devil stopped dancing and glared like a bull about to charge. 'Terrytop!' repeated Duffy. 'Deny that if you can, my fine hellish gentleman!'

At that last word, Terrytop drew himself up, adjusted his coat about his shoulders, and made his last bow. 'A gentleman', he said suavely, 'will never deny his name. I did not expect to be defeated by anyone as unladylike as you; but I assure you, the pleasure of your company is merely postponed, not abandoned.'

With which, he stamped smartly upon the floor and vanished in a puff of sulphurous smoke. All over the house, the knitting turned to ashes; and out on the moors, Squire Lovel found himself naked but for his shoes. Hunt tells us that as the Droll-tellers told it, the story rambled on and ended indelicately. Unfortunately he provides no clues, but it had something to do with the Old Squire and Duffy's young lover.

A jolly enough romp of a fireside tale, and indeed it was sometime performed like a pantomime at Christmas, in the old farmsteads. As I say, the basic plot is to be found in other countries far from the Penwith peninsula. But what gives this version its distinctively Cornish accent – apart from the names and places – is the detail about the witches' sabbath in the Fugoe Hole (or fogou). Elsewhere, the demon is usually spied alone in the woods, dancing round his fire and gleefully singing his name. But it was taken for granted in Penwith that the Devil would appear to keep company with his witches, and that they would meet to enjoy his favours in the Fugoe Hole. If I guess rightly, what Terrytop was whirling about his head in this sadistic orgy was not a forked tail but a bull's pizzle, and he went a good deal further than merely kicking the witches. Perhaps fogous had always been used for such purposes.

This sort of witchcraft clearly went back to the hunting and herding peoples, and much of the energy of the Church, when it came to Cornwall, must have gone into stamping out or transforming their rituals. In many ways it is a pity that the two were regarded as opposed and that Christianity found it so hard to celebrate fertility and sexuality as among the blessings of the Creator. In spite of Plough Monday, Rogation Days and the Harvest Festival, the impression was made that Christianity was the very opposite of the Old Religion; and so it followed that the old powers might be acquired by reversing Christian procedures. There is an interesting case on record to confirm this. In 1841, the *West Briton* reported the example of a witch who had initiated herself by attending Holy Communion, repeating the Lord's Prayer three times backwards, swallowing the wine, but saving the bread and feeding it to a toad. She was detected by a male witch-finder and blamed for causing the deaths of an unspecified number of people.

The Church had only itself to blame, also, if Penwith became a celebrated haunting-ground for the damned, for what with its neglect of the souls of St Buryan and its readiness to deny God's mercy elsewhere, it is a wonder Penwithians had any confidence in salvation at all. I have already mentioned Wild Harris of Kenegie, and Bottrell has a further tale of the man and place, which must qualify as the most horrific of all.

Harris, it appears, made life a misery for his next-of-kin long after he was dead. Usually accompanied by his favourite hound he would career across the downs in demonic chase, stand glaring down the road at the main entrance, or loiter on the steps of the summerhouse where he had imprisoned his unfortunate victim. Eventually it was decided that his spirit must be exorcized, and a famous ghost-layer – the Reverend Mr Polkingthorn of St Ives – was engaged for the task. There is, in fact, a farm called *Polkinghorne* not far from Kenegie.

On the appointed night, a number of local clergy assembled to watch the ceremony, and, as a storm was coming on, took shelter in the summerhouse to await the exorcist. Polkingthorn was late in coming, and one of the more impatient curates foolishly experimented with a formula to summon up spirits. The effect was awful. An icy chill swept through the room, and a tall figure in a long black cloak and a plumed hat stood before the fireplace. Thunder and lightning exploded above their heads, and the little house was besieged by scores of black buccas in pursuit of Wild Harris's spectre. Just as the clergymen were resigning themselves to the worst, the stamp of riding boots and the crack of a whip could be heard outside as Polkingthorn drove off the buccas and forced his way into the room.

'In nomine Domini,' he adjured the ghost, 'I command thee to stay.' Then, drawing a circle around it on the dusty floor, he addressed it in Latin and brought it to its knees before him. Next producing a halter of hempen cord, Polkingthorn lassoed the ghost about the chest and bade it 'In nomine Domini' to follow him, breaking open the magic circle with his foot as he did so. Through the break the spirit glided and meekly followed the exorcist into the garden. Seeing that all the buccas were fled, Polkingthorn released the spirit and asked what disturbed its rest. With unusual conscientiousness the spectre replied that it owed certain small debts which had not been paid, omissions which, it was assured, would speedily be set right. There remained now the problem of binding the ghost to some perpetual task. Up the hill they went together to the summit of Castel-an-Dinas. And there, within the circle of the ramparts, Wild Harris was charged for all Eternity to count the blades of grass. Some say he is counting still, others that his patience was no longer than Tregeagle's and that he is back on his infernal hunt, with the buccas at his heels. This end of the story melts into one of the old myths of the giants and the howling of the wind. At least I am convinced by experience that, if there ever was an exorcism at Kenegie summerhouse, the results have been entirely satisfactory.

One of the pleasures of Penwith legends is that you can read them with a map at your elbow, and then go and see where they happened. A striking example of this – and another ghostly one – is what Hunt titles 'The Spectre Bridegroom', and it is set, appropriately, in St Buryan.

Long ago, it is said, there lived at Boscean a farmer called Lenine. Lenine is a corruption of Lanyon, but Boscean is clearly marked as such on the green-covered Ordnance Survey map – a farm on the eastern lip of the Penberth valley. Lenine had a single son named Frank, and Mrs Lenine was assisted in her household duties by a pretty young girl called Nancy Trenoweth. In short, they fell in love; but Lenine considered her not good enough for his son, and so Nancy was sent home to her parents who lived only a couple of miles inland at Alsia Mill. That, too, is easily found on the map, though it must be Lower Alsia, for that is where the mill still stands. In the last few years, incidentally, the place has been transformed into one of the most tranquil nooks in the peninsula, thanks to the building and gardening activities of the painter and his wife who have come to live there.

Two miles present no sort of barrier to determined young lovers. Hardly an evening passed when Frank did not desert Boscean to ride across country to Alsia. Hunt says the Holy Well was their favourite trysting place, and I must confess I had almost lost faith in the old antiquarian, for although there was a well marked clearly on all the maps, I could not find it. And then the painter at the mill showed me: you go up the hill from the mill a hundred yards, round the corner, across the first field on the left, and halfway along the right-hand edge of the second. And there it is, and sometimes it has votive rags blowing on the hedge overhead. The story says the couple also exchanged vows on the Logan Rock and halved a wedding ring taken from the finger of a corpse.

The outdoor life took its course, until Nancy's parents became aware that what their daughter urgently needed was not half a ring but a whole one, bestowed in the parish church. Farmer Lenine, however, would hear nothing of the alliance, and to prevent its being solemnized carried his son off to Plymouth and signed him on to an East Indiaman. The baby was born soon, but fatherless.

Probably to hide her shame, Nancy left the child with her parents and went back to domestic service. This time she found a place at 'Kimyall' in Paul parish. There are, in fact, three varieties of Kemyel on the map, south of Paul; but I choose Kemyel Wartha because it best fits Hunt's description of it as a village with a town-place, or village green. This green is essential to the story, for one All Souls' Eve it became the scene of a hemp-sowing. The process was simple and often no more than a pre-arranged game: a girl would step forth, scattering hemp seed and crying:

> *Hemp seed I sow,*
> *Hemp seed I hoe;*
> *And he who will my true love be*
> *Come after me and mow.*

And, if her intention had been well enough advertised, her young man would leap out from behind a hedge and walk after her, acting out the reaping. But on this occasion, Nancy and her two girl companions were astonished to see an apparition of Frank Lenine, dripping wet and scowling furiously. Their screams broke the spell, so that next morning they doubted what they had seen.

As the month of November progressed the autumn gales blew up. One cataclysmic night, a great ship from the Indies was thrown against Bernowhall (now Burnewhall) Cliff and shattered. All the crew perished, save one, and that was Frank Lenine. Yet even he had only a few hours' life in him. They carried him over the fields to nearby Boscean, where with his dying breath he recounted a weird story of having been drawn out of his body while he was still at sea and briefly set down in the village of Kemyel. The experience had almost driven him mad, and if ever he could lay hands on the one who had wrought such a spell, he would make her suffer too.

Then he asked for Nancy, to wed her before he died. But still his father would not hear of it, and Frank gave up the ghost in double agony.

None of this reached the ears of Nancy, who was still in service at Kemyel. On the night after her lover had been laid to rest in Buryan churchyard, she was about to lock the door of the house as usual, when a horseman came riding up the lane and called to her in a voice that made her heart leap. It was Frank, mounted upon the horse which had borne him so often to Alsia, and though his voice sounded different – as if there was earth in his mouth – it spoke the message she had longed to hear all those years: 'Climb up behind me, and come where I lie.'

When she took Lenine's hand to mount it was cold as marble, though; and when she passed her arm about his waist, it froze like ice. The cloak against which she pressed her face was damp and musty, and never a word more spoke the rider as they clattered off down the lanes. The route they took is too vaguely described to be certain, though we know that they crossed the Lamorna stream at Trove Bottom where, glancing at their reflection in the water, Nancy saw the full horror of her fate: that was no cloak against her face but a shroud, and this was not her living Frank but his corpse that she grasped. She was being carried to where he lay – buried.

It is my guess that they went by Boleit (the Field of Blood) and the circle of the Dawns Men, and entered Buryan churchtown by the southeasterly lane. But the vital clue is that they rode by the smithy, whose forge was still burning, and that the blacksmith rushed out to save Nancy. This might appear to indicate the westerly lane from Treen, which is quite a different direction, for on the outskirts of Buryan there is still a cottage called 'The Old Forge'. But this lane makes nonsense for anyone riding from Trove. The explanation is, I fancy, that Buryan has had more than one forge and at that time there was one on the road I favour. Indeed, there is still a likely building in the proper place, used until lately for the closely allied purpose of repairing farm machinery.

Out rushed the smith, then, in answer to Nancy's cry, with

a red-hot iron in one hand. With the other he grabbed at the girl's sleeve and pulled her from the horse's back. But the phantom seized the skirt of her dress as she fell, and the two of them were dragged along the ground towards the churchyard. Desperately the smith regained his legs, reached out with his iron and burnt through the dress below the grasping hand. As Nancy dropped clear, the horse leapt the churchyard wall and its rider melted into the freshly piled earth where, a few hours earlier, the mortal remains of Frank Lenine had been interred.

I do not pretend to know where the grave is today. Not far from the church door is a slate gravestone that appeals to me for quite another reason – its splendid example of the art of sombre eulogy:

Francis Hutchen, son of John and Margaret Hutchen, once of this parish was born on the 17th of September 1782 and died on the 15th of July 1812 and was buried in this spot. Reader behold the plainly written page of human life and learn a moral lesson from the life and death of him who sleeps beneath thy feet. This was his native village and here in the playful days of infancy his little feet have pressed the green sward on which thou now standest. Here he grew in activity and strength, foremost of the companions of his youth. His mind and sentiments were cultivated and refined, his heart was kind and affectionate and with those who knew and loved him well he trod hand in hand through the paths of boyhood and manhood, till in the prime of manhood, Death laid him low and those who loved him in life saw him descend into an early grave. He is gone, reader, thy day will come and thou must follow.

It seems to me that if you are going to have epitaphs, that is how they should be written: you don't get a decent read off a modern tombstone. I can well imagine Old Lenine composing something like that, hypocritically, about his Frank. At any rate our story ends with Nancy dying in the smith's arms, leaving her child to the Lenines, and joining her lover in his grave. Upon which was found the burnt-off hem of her dress. As for the horse, it was heard careering madly across country and was discovered, covered in foam, with its tongue and eyes starting from its head, upon Bernowhall Cliff.

Well, the names are possible and the places real enough. Maybe there was a romance which ended in the boy being sent off to sea, where he was drowned. But I fear the tale is too literary, too Gothic, to be much more real than that. Hunt says it bears a striking resemblance to the 'Lenore' of Bürger, which I have not been able to read, though he doubts whether such a ballad can have found its way to Boscean. Personally, I am not so sure. It is remarkable how stories did circulate, especially with soldiers returning from foreign wars. Good ghost stories were always in demand, and as the eighteenth century moved into the nineteenth they seem to have taken the place of tales about witches and devils. Scientifically minded Victorians were not prepared to entertain the possibility of Black Magic, but they had an uneasy feeling that there might be something after death which was not entirely according to the rules.

To a community which did not yet know the rules and lacked the services of the meteorologist, the Agriculture Department Advisory Service and even the vet, it was perfectly clear that there were malevolent forces at work, often linked with the dead. The Church might claim to understand them and to explain them in terms of man's sinfulness and God's wrath. But where the Church was weak and negligent – where it had lost touch with the country folk by conducting its teaching in a foreign language – those explanations would not carry much weight.

In addition to the mysteries of the landscape, Penwithians lived on two further levels that were even more mysterious: the mines that were under the land and the sea that surrounded it. Both were unpredictable and fraught with violence and death: there are many tales not only of buccas and mermaids, but of once-human spirits chained to their former occupations.

Penwith, like other parts near the sea, has its stories of phantom ships and Flying Dutchmen, and of ships that are seen sailing over the land. Porthcurno has, or had, one that moved up the valley about nightfall, when the mists were rising, rose towards Bodelan (where St Levan used to live) and then towards the farm of Chegwidden, where it vanished like smoke. It was a black, square-rigged boat with a single mast, towing a small dinghy, but not a man was ever seen upon deck. The ghostly craft was thought to have some connection with a retired seafarer who once lived at Cheg-widden, tended only by a sinister foreign servant. They spoke to nobody and one theory was that they were pirates; smugglers too, perhaps, for they kept a boat at Porthcurno and put to sea each day, whatever the weather, only returning at night. They also hunted their own pack of hounds, and we are back with the demon giants when we read that their midnight baying kept the whole countryside awake.

At last the seafarer died, and his coffin was brought over the fields to St Levan churchyard. Round the grave gathered the hounds, with the sinister servant in their midst: yet as soon as the earth fell on the coffin's lid, the mist rolled in, dogs and servant vanished, and the boat too vanished from the cove. And from this day, says Hunt, nobody has been able to keep a boat at Porthcurno.

It is true that they don't, for the beach shelves steeply, there is no shelter or jetty and the waves often run high, forced up by the sandy bottom, as they do all the way to the Logan Rock. Again there may have been a recluse with a negro servant at Chegwidden: Hunt can put no date to the story. But he had met a man who had actually seen the inland boat.

Home in the West

The Cornishman's home is not so much a castle as a granite box. But as Nikolaus Pevsner remarks, while Cornwall may have little of the highest aesthetic quality to reward the architectural scholar, the picturesque traveller will find much that is lovable and even moving. Like most things Cornish, Penwith carries this to extremes. What style there is in its most typical buildings is an absence of style, dictated by hardship – or by the hardship of the life and the hardness of the materials.

Wood can never have been plentiful in these parts and bricks (in spite of the present vogue for pottery) were never baked here; but granite in every shape and size, from elongated slabs to handy chunks, has always lain about the moors or had to be cleared from the fields if any ploughing was to be done. Here and there the slatey killas was a substitute. Neither is easily worked, especially without power-driven cutting equipment, and although you will see elaborate ornamentation on churches like Launceston and Probus further east, Penwith's workmanship is basic and crude. No fancy masons were imported here from Devon: you can almost hear the local lads cursing as they hacked away at their one-piece octagonal pillars and their two-piece arches.

There can never have been much money for building ostentatiously 'To the Glory of God' – St Buryan with its royal foundation excepted – and a kind of standard 'utility' church seems to have developed in the fourteenth and fifteenth centuries with a nave, wagon roof, usually a south aisle, north transept and an unbuttressed tower at the west end, with battlements and pinnacles. The churches seem to grow out of the landscape: they do not impose themselves on it nor fight against it nor shame the parishioners by flaunting a style they cannot afford in their own homes. I have already awarded my prize to St Levan, and parish loyalty must put Zennor high on the list. But I must confess a special affection for tiny thirteenth-century Towednack, pronounced 'Twennock' and named for St Tewinnock the Confessor, whose real name was probably Winnock. His church has an extremely ancient altar stone, retrieved from a hedge, but no pinnacles because the Devil kept knocking them down.

I have said that towns and villages were not part of the old Cornish way of life. People lived dotted about the countryside in a 'tre' (farmstead) or in a 'chy' (house). Which is why every turn in the lane has a name to it. Treen or Treryn is the Hillside Farm, and a spot called Chykembro was the Welshman's House.

There is some reason to believe that the very first people in Penwith kept close to the shore and ate quantities of limpets off the rocks (you can knock them off with your bare hand if you take them by surprise). But the first habitations you can identify are no earlier than a century or two B.C. and were occupied during the late Iron Age, the Roman Occupation and the so-called Dark Ages or early mediaeval times. These were the courtyard house villages, a speciality of Penwith. There are two well-excavated examples under public care at Chysauster (near Newmill between Penzance and the Gurnard's Head) and Carn Euny (best approached from Sancreed in the middle of the peninsula). There is a further example on private farmland just behind Porthmeor, on the Zennor–Morvah road: it is overgrown with gorse and brambles and hard to find, for it merges with the field hedges and has become part of the landscape. The Porthmeor village I find more romantic than the others, for it has fortifications – even a gatehouse – and stands within sight of the sea, like a tiny Troy. Snuggled up to one of the ruins is what the experts consider to be an above-ground fogou, but it does not convince me as that.

The general idea of a courtyard house seems to have been to build a roughly egg-shaped enclosure, with a gate leading into a central yard and various rooms and store-houses looped off and roofed over from the enclosure wall. There was usually a circular living-room with a socket-stone in the middle to take the roof support; the roofing was probably branches and thatch of some kind, turf would have been very heavy. Some of the houses have stone channels running through them, but I doubt if this was a water supply; more likely it was to drain off the slurry from the cattle which shared the courtyards, for while Porthmeor's occupants were well situated to do some tin-streaming, the other villages look more like farming communities. Their way of life seems hardly to have been touched by the Romans, lasting into the fifth and even sixth centuries, when it must have been among the most primitive in England.

Carn Euny, Chysauster and Porthmeor have survived as well as they have largely because of their isolation. Many other sites have been pillaged for stone and more still must have been incorporated into farmsteads which are occupied to this day. Some of the ancient but humble cottages we admire now must have been regarded as grand when they were new, for people like Cherry of Zennor lived in granite hovels with turf stuffed into the cracks and such dwellings could rise and fall literally overnight. As late as the 1830s (when Hunt began noting his tales) the belief persisted that if you got the walls up, the roof on, and a fire burning on the hearth before dawn broke – you were entitled to the freehold of the place for ever. Your chance of getting away with it must have improved with the remoteness of the spot you chose, and many must have been knocked down by angry landowners. But once you were accepted the way was open to extend the original structure or use it as a cowshed and build something better nearby. I know a number of farmyards where something like this can be seen to have happened, at least to the extent that today's cowshed has blocked-up windows and a fireplace that suggest it was yesterday's cottage. And if you look at the end of a cottage, you can often see where the roof has been raised to make a second storey. The typical Cornish barn, however, with its hayloft reached by an outside stair and its hipped roof ochred with lichen, was not (I think) used as a family dwelling with people upstairs and cattle down. Some of the isolated barns on the moors may have been used for sleeping by the herdsman during the summer months – for in some parts there was a kind of alpine system of summer and winter pastures – but they would have been too cold for a family in winter: there is usually no water near and never any fireplace. Only today has it become a favourite exercise for Penzance architects to convert them into homes – which they do with considerable skill now that the planning authorities have withdrawn their opposition to such conversion. One Penwith farmer told me over a glass of beer that he had three cash crops – cows, cauliflowers and barns – and barns, he said sadly, was running out.

Heaving large boulders into position for a cottage was not the kind of thing a squatter could manage overnight, even if he had friends to help him. The average hovel would be built with the size of stones that a man could lift by himself, bound either with turf or 'cob' which was a mixture of mud and chopped straw with chalk (which was hard to find) and slate rubble. The cottage I use is made of a mixture like this, and keeping out the damp is a perpetual battle, won only by cementing the outside and soaking it with a consolidating solution like resin. Even so, the moisture soaks up from the ground and one is constantly killing off the green mould with chlorine and then whitewashing over the stains. Old Corn-wall can have been no place for the rheumaticky, and it is no wonder the old stories were told round the hearth and its built-in oven.

Many cottagers held their properties under a strange sys-tem of leasing based upon human life. An unwanted piece of waste ground would be let at a nominal rent and the tenant would build his own home on it on condition that the land and buildings would revert to the owner upon the death not of the tenant, but of the longest surviving of three other independent persons. Selecting these persons must have been a tricky gamble: children were particularly susceptible to disease, but as we have seen, a man or woman who had survived childhood still had only a short expectation of life ahead. I suppose an anthropologist might explain it in terms of encouraging a community to take tender care of each other, but I cannot help feeling it was a desperate attempt to spread the risks of uncertain fate.

The legends I have been recalling need to be imagined against such a background of uncertainty and discomfort. This was by no means a Christmas card Merrie England, all Cornish cream and cider – proper cream, by the way, was scalded *before* being separated from the milk; and according to one authority, the cider should have a twenty-year-old toad floating in it, always saved for the next brewing. The Penwithians of today are the descendants of great survivors, and perhaps one can forgive them for not wanting to dwell sentimentally on so painful a past. Wilkie Collins, writing in 1860, remarked with enthusiasm that 'In the Government Tables of Mortality for Cornwall there are no returns of death from starvation', that the people were lucky to have inexhaustible treasures of fish and tin to draw upon where agriculture might fail them, and that 'It is impossible not to conclude that the Cornish poor suffer less by their poverty, and enjoy more opportunities of improving their social position, than the majority of their brethren in many other counties of England.' But Collins hit a relatively prosperous time, and one in which – as he admits – the burden of surplus population on the labour market had been reduced by massive emigration. The potato blight had been almost as effective in stimulating an exodus from Cornwall as it had been from Ireland; added to which, Cornwall could export skilled miners to the goldfields of Australia and America. By 1867 they were doling out free bread and soup to almost 700 'half starved men and women' in Redruth, and the *West Briton* observed that the poor were beginning to show 'prominent marks of suffering'.

It is no exaggeration to say that life for the Droll-tellers' audience was nasty, brutish and short. There was a bullbaiting in Penzance in 1814. In 1819 the mayor of Bodmin, 'lately much infested by vagrants', ordered them to be flogged through the streets. In 1826 a French merchantman was wrecked on Hayle Bar and plundered by the neighbouring villagers with all the old, drunken gusto – some of the men knocking in the heads of wine barrels and drinking out of

ABOVE: *Zennor, Moorstones*
BELOW: *St Michael's Mount*

ABOVE: *Treen Castle, Logan Rock in the middle*

BELOW: *Lamorna, Merry Maidens*

Botallack, ruined gateway

LEFT: *Crows-an-Wra, the Witch Cross*
BELOW: *Newlyn, fishing fleet*
OPPOSITE ABOVE: *Rosemorran, the Monk's Porch*
OPPOSITE BELOW: *Trewoofe, back right, remains of manor*

ABOVE: *Carnelloe, cliff pinnacles*
LEFT: *Tresco Abbey gardens*
BELOW: *St Mary's, chambered tomb*

their hats. In 1838, one Joseph Perryman was sentenced to seven years transportation for stealing a black hen *at night* (which was considered a special threat to property), and at the same assizes a boy of fifteen was ordered to be transported for life after stealing a basket, on the grounds that it was his second offence. The stocks were still in use at Hayle in 1862, and in Camborne four years later; while Cornwall's last public hanging was witnessed by thousands as late as 1862. Two young women presented themselves at Bodmin jail, asking if they might be touched by the dead hand of the convict, that being known as a sure cure for sore necks. There was always a lively demand for pieces of the rope used at a hanging.

And there were food riots, inter-parish affrays and frequent drunken brawls – for until about 1870 the area was peppered with common drinking houses or Tiddlywinks. Things might have been very much worse but for the vigilance of the excisemen and the sobering influence of Methodism. There also seem to have been surprisingly few strikes, and on at least one occasion West Cornwall miners were sent up to Sunderland as strike-breakers, and on another granite-masons were advertised for to take over from those who had refused to go on building Trafalgar Square.

It is hard now to think of Penwith as an industrial area. Even in the high days of mining its blows must have been softened by the sea on one side and the farms on the other. Only in Pendeen and St Just do you catch glimpses of the rows of mean cottages that recall South Wales or the North of England. Perhaps if there was more squalor in sight and more parliamentary seats to be won, Penwith's scandalous unemployment would attract greater sympathy from London. Her mines, though, were always far more vulnerable to foreign alternatives than the coal-mines of Britain, open-and-shut cases almost throughout the nineteenth century. But for the shutting, we should be cursing them today as environmental pollution, instead of rhapsodizing about those stern, chapel-like silhouettes against the skyline.

Tin was first panned from the streams of Penwith before the Romans came. Some time in the Middle Ages, people began following veins of ore into the cliff faces from the shore line; you can find horizontal adits of this kind between St Ives and Cape Cornwall (but take care!). The advantage of this type of mining is that, provided you keep the tunnel sloping downhill towards the entrance, it will drain itself, whereas any kind of vertical shaft is going to call for a pump.

The old tin-streamers and shallow-diggers were literally a law to themselves, for under Richard I's Stannaries Charter they were free to search anywhere they liked for tin, subject only to their own stannary courts and parliament. (Attempts have been made to secure Cornish self-government by invoking stannary privilege, but if I were you I should not accept a stannary pound note or try taking a stannary car licence onto the M4.) The tin, once smelted, had to be stamped and taxed at one of the coinage towns – originally Lostwithiel, Liskeard, Truro and Helston; but as the tin in the east became harder to get the working shifted westwards, and in 1663 Penzance became an authorized centre. But still tinning was largely a matter of small groups of men prowling the moors and streams, sleeping out in the moor-houses or bothies and passing their nights round a furze fire telling the old legends. In a way, they were the last of Tregeagle's companions.

Two things happened to revolutionize the stannaries. The first was the realization, with deeper digging, that beneath the alluvial tin which was brought in by the pound lay lodes of copper that could be extracted by the ton, far and away the richest then known in the world. By 1750, copper had easily surpassed tin as the gold of Cornwall, and it was put into men's hands by the second development: the invention of the big atmospheric steam pump which came into action in the Redruth district. The whole scale of mining was now far beyond the individual tinner and manageable only by capitalist organization.

As the mines went deeper, the life of the working man became harder, more dangerous, less healthy. Often he had to climb up and down a thousand feet or more of vertical ladders, for lift cages were a very late and rare luxury. One extraordinary device was the 'man engine', with notches cut into the sides of an enormous wooden rod which rose and fell

all the way down the shaft from the engine on the surface.
The miner stepped onto a notch and was lowered with the
down-stroke of the engine. As it reached the bottom of its
stroke, he stepped off onto a step in the wall of the shaft. The
rod rose again on the up-stroke, and at the top of that the
miner stepped back onto the rod to be lowered several feet
more. On one side of the rods were miners ascending, on the
other miners going down: it must have been like something
out of Dante, and on one occasion – at the old Levant mine,
near Geevor, in 1919 – the rods broke and 31 men were
dashed to their deaths in the pit.

I won't make this a history of the Penwith mining industry,
of how the copper was killed by the discovery of deposits in
Chile, Australia and America, how tin revived when it was
found underneath the copper lodes, and how that too was
killed by the Australian and Malayan discoveries. Every
Cornishman knows there is still tin down there if only
someone had the courage to invest in it, but by 1881 the *West
Briton* was saying 'Every tourist in Cornwall is familiar with
the deserted engine-houses and ruinous chimney stacks which
form so characteristic a feature of the western mining dis-
tricts. They have their picturesque aspects, but they are
evidences of widespread ruin . . . Millions drawn from the
wealth and the poverty of outside investors have within the
past 30 years been buried in the bowels of the Cornish
hills . . .'.

They stand there still, stripped of everything portable or
saleable, sometimes (as at Bosigran) a pair of them standing at
right angles to one another across a single shaft. One, the
smaller, would have housed the whim-engine which raised
the ore, while the larger house would have contained the
pumping engine. What accounts for the massive construction
of these engine-houses is that they were actually *part* of the
engine, which was firmly bolted to them, and had to act as a
counterweight to (perhaps) a thousand feet of 12-inch square
rods. And these rods were attached to a rocking beam or
'bob' which could weigh thirty or forty tons and which rested
on a huge block of granite overlooking the shaft, known as
the bob wall. Anyone who admires steam would have had his

breath taken away by the sight of one of these majestic monsters operating flat out at ten strokes a minute. We shall not look upon their like again, now that diesel and electricity have taken over; but you can see the real thing grinding away at East Pool, between Camborne and Redruth, thanks to the preservationists, and a stirring sight it is, too.

At the back of the engine-house, usually at one corner, like the campanile of a cathedral, stands the chimney stack – granite two-thirds the way up, topped with brick. It carried off the sulphurous smoke from the boiler, a piece of apparatus that sometimes became a social centre, with men drying wet clothes by it, women fetching buckets of hot water from it or doing their laundry and even ingeniously employing waste steam to cook things. Occasionally a boiler would explode with ghastly results; and there was one at Wheal Vor near Helston which was haunted by a plague of little black dogs after mangled flesh from two underground casualties had been hastily shovelled into the furnace.

To remove the unpleasant taste of that story, let me recommend a visit to the engine-houses at Ding Dong and Greenburrow, on the roof of the world northwest of New-mill. Ding Dong is said to have been worked since Roman times (which seems improbable), but its great days were from 1814 to 1878, with unsuccessful attempts at revival in 1912 and 1928. People have kept trying to reopen Cornish mines, whenever the price of tin soared, but either the price has collapsed again, or else the working costs have proven uneconomic. Botallack closed in the 1890s, reopened in 1907 and finally shut in 1914; while Giew, whose engine-house stands beside the B3311 near the Engine Inn, was closed once in 1867 and again in 1923.

There really is a Ding Dong bell, and you can see it inside the church at Madron. There is a 'legend' that Our Lord came to Ding Dong with Joseph of Arimathea, looking for tin (for they say that Ding Dong was old when the Romans came here); but I don't believe a word of it. I think it is a Victorian pious fraud, part of the Glastonbury nonsense. There are no mediaeval traces of it, and can anyone believe that if the early Celtic Church had got wind of it they would have failed to

make the most of it, with shrines and holy wells and chapels?
As it is, the most important holy visitor commemorated is St
Michael the Archangel, of St Michael's Mount.

Along the skyline to the west of Ding Dong stands the
engine-house of Greenburrow, like the last castle between
Heaven and Earth, its granite blocks slammed and wedged
together with an Inca massiveness. It has a chimney like a
lighthouse, with the wind hissing round it, and from its
ramparts you can look out towards Land's End in one
direction, across moors dabbed with the colours of heather
and gorse, or over Mount's Bay in the other. There are
theories about using the mines to tap the heat below the
earth's crust as a new source of energy, but, myself, I would
feel it a kind of violation of the dead if anyone tried to shock
these shafts into life again. They have known so much
exploitation, so much bravery and suffering. If you seek a
monument to the miners of Penwith, stand at Greenburrow
and look around you.

The decay of the mines and the emigration of so many
Cornish miners has been largely responsible for the surplus of
Methodist chapels in the peninsula. Abandoned, they are
awkward things to deal with, too lofty to convert easily into
dwellings. Some have become barns, other builders' stores,
and the one at Carfury near Ding Dong – where Isobel Baillie
once sang – has been ingeniously adapted as a workshop
below and, above, a flat of the most glorious aspects and
considerable comfort. It is tempting to dream up schemes for
turning them into concert rooms or art galleries: but who
would visit them outside the tourist season, and who is to
provide the art and the music to go in them and at what price?
In Pevsner's words, there is not much in them to reward the
architectural scholar – even the opera houses like Hayle and St
Just – so I fear we can hardly expect any public body to
preserve them for their own sakes. They would not even
make very picturesque ruins. I know of one which was
bought with a view to fitting holiday flats into the shell but,
as so often, planning complications appear to have thwarted
the scheme. A pity, this, for surely it is better that car workers
from Coventry should help to keep the roof on than that the

hymns and prayers of the departed should have no memorial but a heap of rubble.

Penwith has enough heaps of rubble, and they are no less regrettable when cleared away. The one I would soonest see restored – and it vanished as late as the mid-1930s – was the manor house of Trewoofe (pronounced 'Trove') at the top of the Lamorna valley. Bottrell, who knew it when it was still standing, though divided, compares it to Avalon and tells of it a legend which is both ancient and (again) temptingly operatic.

On the west wall of St Buryan church, near the font, is a monument to Arthur Levelis (rhymes with 'the trellis'), erected in 1671. It reads:

> *This worthy family hath flourished here*
> *Since William's conquest full six hundred year*
> *And longer much it might, but that the blest*
> *Must spend their seavenths in a blessed rest*
> *But yet this gentleman last of his name*
> *Hath by his virtues eternised the same*
> *Much more than children could or bookes for love*
> *Records it here in hearts, in life above.*

(I take it that 'seavenths' or sevenths refers to the sabbath or day of rest.)

The Levelises were the Lovels of Duffy and the Devil, and they lived at Trewoofe for at least 400 years (if not 600) having married into the 'de Trewoofe' family, the 'Troves de Trove'. Levelis is clearly a Norman name, too, but the Domesday Book is very sketchy on Cornwall and the slovenly administration of the Deanery does not help either. There is no documentary reference to the de Trewoofes before 1270. But in 1302 Thomas de Trewoofe granted his mother and her *second* husband various properties at a rent of one rose annually, and Thomas was one of those excommunicated over the disgraceful fracas in Buryan churchyard. He backed the King's party against the Bishop's, and it is interesting that when Bishop Grandisson delivered his vindictive sermon he gave it in Latin which had to be translated into

French, English and Cornish, to make sure that everyone understood him. It says something for the ability of the Saxons, Normans and Celts to coexist in the Land's End peninsula; and, in a way, they still do – upcountrymen, foreigners and natives.

There is no point in chronicling here the entire known history of the Trewoofe estate. One interesting detail is that in 1413 the 'de Trewoofes' were granted the bishop's licence for a private chapel. The bishop himself could not be bothered – or did not dare – to come and consecrate it on the spot, but a portable altar-stone (after the Celtic fashion) was sent to him for blessing. It seems that a private chapel was the fashionable thing for a considerable house to acquire (there was another at Trembethow, near Trencrom), and although Trewoofe's is no more to be seen there is still a field overlooking it which is known as 'Round Park Chapel', where pieces of carved stone have been unearthed.

The last of the de Trewoofes had six daughters and divided up his property between them. Somehow the youngest, who married Thomas Levelis, got the house and from then on it was rebuilt into an E-shaped Elizabethan manor with a massive doorway in the centre, facing down the Lamorna valley, surmounted by the coats of arms of the two families. This doorway still survives in the garden of a house in St Ives, and it would be appropriate if it were brought back some day. Other bits and pieces of Tudor Trewoofe have been incorporated in the buildings which now occupy the site.

Thomas had two sons, Hugh and John, of whom John lived to inherit the place. He in turn was succeeded by a son, Arthur, who is shown on a map of 1604 as then being in occupation. Arthur's heir was another Hugh (a name worth remembering), and so it goes on until the extinction of the Levelis line in 1671, after which we find Vospers, Leaks, Tremewans, Harveys and Bosustows. The second Hugh Levelis may have been involved in an episode during the Civil War, in which a troop of Royalists were hidden in the Fugoe Hole until their Parliamentary pursuers had gone.

Today, Trewoofe is a secret oasis among the trees. All that remains of the manor is a square block that was once the east wing of the E. It contains a massive granite fireplace going back to the seventeenth century and some tiny windows that look even older. There are other buildings dotted about containing borrowed granite door and window frames, and overlooking the dell a mid-eighteenth-century house which the Bosustows built using material from the west wing. It is mildly haunted by unexplained footsteps.

Trewoofe, as a once considerable estate, has various out-lying properties. As you take a sharp bend on the B3315 from Newlyn you pass the older Clapper Mill, where Duffy had a companion in Old Bet, the witch. Up a lane on to the high ground above the Bosustow house is the classic barn of Grambla, which is probably early seventeenth century. And if you make your way courteously through the Trewoofe group and leftwards down the track towards the valley, you pass the easily identifiable sites of the orchards, rabbit warren and vegetable plots and can look over the gate of a most beautiful stream-fed garden where the pigeon-house once stood. Delightfully, the owners still keep pigeons.

The driveway to the Bosustow house crosses the leat that leads down towards the mill. The little bridge at the entrance to the drive looks on to a marshy enclosure that was once the millpond, and this is the focal point of the story I wish to tell: for it was haunted. Haunted by the spirits of two beautiful children, a boy and a younger girl, who were to be seen hand in hand picking flowers on the margins of the pool or hovering over the water.

This is the tale as Bottrell tells it. Long ago, Trewoofe was left to a young (alas, unnamed) Levelis son who was placed under the guardianship of his uncle, one *Hugh* Levelis. The boy was apprenticed squire to a knight in some distant part of the country and in due course went off to the Crusades. Nothing was heard of him for years – there were even rumours that he had been slain by the Muhammadans – and Hugh Levelis, who had diligently farmed the estate, began to believe that Trewoofe was rightly his. Then, without warn-ing, the heir returned as a fully-fledged knight, bringing with him, a fair lady, two children and a dusky maidservant.

At first the uncle resisted the knight's claim to Trewoofe.

But it was proved, the marriage was blessed in Buryan church, and Hugh retreated to a position of subservience – a calculated manoeuvre, it would seem, for the call of the wars eventually proved too strong for the knight. Bottrell describes how the fever of the holy wars swept the land, how Sir Levelis responded to it with joy and urged the peasantry to follow his banner to Jerusalem; how they shouldered their picks and pitchforks, packed their pouches with pasties and got (some of them) as far as the Tamar. Upon learning this was not the River Jordan, and that even Exeter was not the Holy City, most of them turned back. But a handful of them marched on and a smaller handful still did arrive in Palestine.

Back in Lamorna valley, something like the story of Penelope was repeating itself. Hugh Levelis reasserted himself in the hall, but the Lady withdrew to her bower where she and her maid busied themselves with exotic needlework. In particular, 'they worked from first daylight until dark, making a piece of tapestry in which was portrayed the lifelike image of the absent knight, arrayed in his glittering armour with sword in hand, just as he had appeared when setting out for the wars.'

This tapestry was hung over the door to the Lady's chamber; but as she meant it to be a surprise for her husband's return, it was covered by a plain curtain.

The logic of time pressed home. Uncle Hugh was not an ill-looking man, and at length the Lady accepted the inevitable: that her knight had perished in battle and that she should marry the one who had so faithfully and uncomplainingly tended his estate. There was some difficulty about marrying a deceased husband's father's brother, but the church was recompensed for finding a way round it (here Bottrell gives a nudge and a wink about Mother Church's venal ways) and the wedding day arrived. It arrived and left: for the wedding guests spent the whole of it searching in vain for the two children, who had vanished without trace.

There follows a dramatic scene in which Hugh Levelis forces his way into the Lady's bedchamber, she flees, he grabs at her dress but seizes instead the doorway curtain which falls, bringing him face to face with the glaring tapestry of the knight. The sight of this ghastly vision – surely the spirit of his nephew come with sword in hand to defend his wife's virtue – so terrifies the uncle that he leaps from the chamber window and is never seen again.

Dawn breaks, and the Lady looks sorrowfully down from her window. There in the garden she sees a travel-stained figure: it is, of course, Sir Levelis, home for good from the Crusades, and the story he has to tell lays further woe over her joy.

The knight is now sickened with the meaningless slaughter he has witnessed; disillusioned at the lies and hypocrisy of the Church. He and his companions acquitted themselves like true sons of Cornwall in battle – One for All and All for One – but they were taken prisoner by the Saracens, who, to their astonishment, treated them with greater chivalry than they had seen amongst the ranks of the Crusaders. Far from being tortured or humiliated, they were told that they might be ransomed or exchanged, and but for the fact that their honour would not allow them to be purchased for too low a price, they might have been freed earlier.

A few days after being set at liberty, Levelis was riding once more over the field of battle to see if anything could be found of his former comrades. The thought of them conjured up a great longing for home when, suddenly, his horse started, and looking up the knight saw floating towards him from the west the apparition of a boy and girl, surrounded by leaves and apparently floating in water. The boy held the girl by the hand, while the other grasped a green hazel twig. She bore a garland of wild flowers, and together they beckoned the horseman to follow them into the sunset.

He knelt and recited the *Pater Noster*, then the *Ave Maria*, and as he reached the words 'now, and at the hour of our death', the children nodded and floated away. There was no doubt what he was to do.

Levelis and his three ransomed friends made their way to the coasts of Tyre and Sidon where they found a ship bound for Market-Jew for tin. Exhausted though he was by the voyage, the knight set foot immediately for Trewoofe and was greeted on arrival by the same phantom children with the twig and the flowers in their hands, who glide before him and vanish over the mill-pool.

At once the miller is summoned and the pool drained. Close in under one bank the bodies of the children are found, the boy still tightly grasping his sister with one hand, while the other clutches the hazel branch, broken in his last struggle to draw her out . . .

Well, tales of wicked uncles are not uncommon – though there is no record of any such manoeuvres among the Levelises. In spite of the epitaph's claim that they had been in St Buryan since the conquest, the original Thomas Levelis actually came from Castle Horneck, a site outside Penzance. The Levelises may have been Crusaders, but it seems unlikely they set out from Trewoofe. And there are other anachronisms. Bottrell's description of the people setting off in a rabble for the Holy Land sounds like the First Crusade, the so-called People's Crusade 1095, whipped up by Peter the Hermit and Walter the Penniless. But the English played little part in this, and anyway – how could the knight already have been on a *previous* crusade? Perhaps he was one of the English mercenaries hired by the Byzantine Emperor Alexius Comnenus. But this way, I think, lies confusion. The Crusades went on into the early 1300s and there must have been enough cases of knights coming home like Odysseus to discover hanky panky in the boudoir for the plot to become a standard. Droll-tellers in later centuries would not have bothered their heads with historical exactitude. The nearest Bottrell's informant gets is a glancing reference to 'the Jerusalem wars and the days of old King John'. So I do not think the Crusader setting, or the tapestry, are excuses for applying the Alfred-and-the-cakes theory. But I think the drowned children are. Once again, there is no record that any small Levelises *did* perish in the mill-pond, but families at Trewoofe were large, mortality was high and we do not know the cause of death for most of them. I believe that two children *were* drowned in that way, in their father's absence, and that he may have had a dream about them. What better way could there have been of warning later generations from the water's edge than to perpetuate their tragedy in a legend?

Hayle and Farewell

Less than a mile from where I was brought up, in West Hertfordshire, is a grassy ride known as Cherry Bounce. Halfway along it, at the edge of a wood, is a deep pit called Poll Redding's Dell Hole. Poll Redding was a witch who was buried there with a stake through her heart; but if you ran round the dell three times and called 'Poll Redding, come out!' – she would come out, or so my father said. I passed this on to my own children, and they managed two-and-a-half circuits before bolting in terror.

Who is to say that Poll Redding is less real than Augustus Smith (see page 150), or that centuries from now they will not be telling equally fantastic stories about him? My point is that every part of England has seen its legendary events, and that a myth is not necessarily a fairy story, not all of it. The richness of Penwith is that so many of its legends have come down to us, and that if we can breathe life into them, they can breathe life into the country we see.

Even if some of my reconstructions are fanciful, the myths are still true in spirit – they still correspond to certain ages of man. The giants, for example, take us back to the arrival of the very first men in Cornwall: who had made this landscape, who had piled these massive stacks of rock one upon another up on the moors and hilltops? In due course, they became merged with the Celtic robber barons who took over the hilltops. And when the giant Bolster (from the Cornish 'bol', meaning 'an axe') took his six-mile stride from the Beacon to Carn Brea, it was symbolic of how a chieftain had moved his camp from one hilltop to another. The giants, as I say, came before the Gods; they were unruly forces that not even the Druids could systematize, and it is implied that Tregeagle, with his endless labouring at sandbars, was himself a giant. Penwith may look small on the map, but when you are standing on the cliffs or the moors, you feel yourself at the mercy of gigantic forces. And there are few places in the British Isles where the gales blow harder or the waves come in with a longer reach across the Atlantic.

When the organized gods came to Cornwall, they were probably Celtic gods, and it is a pity they have left very few specific legends. Perhaps they lie hidden behind some of the place-names, certainly they were worshipped in the stone circles which may have been built partly to make up for the absence of natural groves of trees. The Devil – who *did* come to Cornwall – is horned because he is really the Celtic herd-god Cernunnos; and Arthur, even if he was a real figure, is a typical Celtic demi-god like Cuchulainn. The extinct Cornish chough, a kind of crow, was said to embody the spirit of Arthur, and we know that the raven was sacred to the Celts.

But the mythology of the Druids was vigorously suppressed by the Christian Church. The age of the saints must have been an age of brainwashing, with many Druidic sites and structures being adapted to the new faith. I guess that the wells are probably the most lasting examples, for they are often in strange places that make little sense in relation to the parish churches. The saints who came up the Hayle estuary from Ireland or Wales clearly did not find any wealthy lords to endow their foundations; they were among the humblest saints in Britain, and today it is the humbleness of their churches that is so appealing.

But if organized religion managed to drive out the giants it had a much more difficult time with the Little People and the spirits of the dead. It has to be admitted that giants are, *prima facie*, hard to believe in, if only because there can never have been anyone who had actually seen one, and nothing that could be mistaken for one. But a seal could be a mermaid – seals are not easily caught, and I have never heard that the Cornish ate them – and there was plenty of evidence for the existence of Little People, even if they were elusive. How else to account for things disappearing, going mysteriously wrong, turning out other than they should – all kinds of things, like changelings, that the Church could not account for? And there is that wistful, heart-breaking legend of the souls of the unbaptized getting smaller and smaller and finally turning into ants. The age of the Little People, which lingered on into the nineteenth century, illustrates the reluctance of a people who had once understood the world in terms of nature spirits to interpret it in terms of scientific laws.

The Celts believed in a life after death – apparently without the punishments of Hell. This must have presented a severe problem to the Christian Church, which had quite a different theory. It must have been necessary for the saints and their successors to have emphasized the penalties of sin and to have painted the sufferings of the damned and the unbaptized in the most lurid of colours. It is this tradition, I think, which kept stories like Tregeagle and The Phantom Bridegroom alive and for which the Church had only itself to blame. For if the souls of the damned are denied their rest and excluded from Heaven, it is small wonder if they come back to warn us and plague us, and express their discomfort in a comfortless landscape.

Dolf Rieser, the veteran etcher who used to live at Bosporthennis, above Porthmeor, called it the strongest landscape in England. It is strong because under its taut muscles you can see its very bones; there is no spare fat on it. It is unpadded, uncluttered, almost wholly without ornament. You become aware, especially in winter, of its underlying structure and of its relationship with the sea and sky that enclose it, and of its textures. Heather, bracken, gorse and blackthorn mantle it closely like coarse tweed, and the stone hedges chop it up into tiny principalities some of which have been there since the Iron Age. These hedges serve the double purpose of breaking the wind and getting the rocks off the land.

The rock keeps breaking through to the surface. It cannot be kept down below, where it belongs, for it is mostly of the violent fiery kind. It likes to crawl out on to the moors and carns and bask there in the sun, letting the wind and rain carve it into fanciful shapes. And down below lie the copper and tin.

Whether granite or greenstone, the cliffs of Penwith are far from being passive and dead. I have contemplated them for hours from a point between the Gurnard's Head and Zennor Cliff and marvel at their architecture, at the great lines of force running up through them carrying the strains and stresses down to their foundations. Before you, you can *see* the curvature of the horizon, and at your feet the sudden drop down to the water leaves you with space into which your imagination – your sense of dance, even of flight – can fling itself. Close at hand a granite fence-post; then the chasm of Porth Glaze; then Boswednack Cliff; and in the distance the sphinx-like crouch of Carn Galver – give you a rare perspective of near, middle, far and very far distance, with gulls and fulmars demonstrating the use of it.

There are any number of places where you can trap such a vision. Even Land's End has its moments but less spoiled is the Logan Rock and the beach of Pednevounder, which you reach from Treen. To get to them you have a choice: outside the car park (thoughtfully provided at the top of the village) is a charming chapel-of-ease dated 1839. Standing with your back to it, you can either march straight ahead over a stile and across the fields to the Logan Rock, or take the right hand along a rough lane that brings you out onto the clifftop. Pednevounder means 'the head at the end of the lane'. Arrived there, you join the path half-right, and turn left at the *second* buttress of rocks to descend onto Cornwall's most splendid beach: but you must consult the tide-tables, because it is inaccessible at high water. Unfortunately its popularity has risen with the years, but numbers will always be kept down by the arduousness of the scramble to reach it. If you doubt your heart or your legs, the Logan Rock is easier. The path over the fields brings you directly to the triple ramparts that defend the neck of the headland, and once over them you can scramble through a whole ruined city of crags and blocks, in the midst of which stands the unrockable Rock itself.

But there is a more discreet and charming experience to be had while you are at Treen. Leaving your car in the village, descend onto the main road and keep hard right: this is the lane to Penberth, and though it is possible to drive most of the

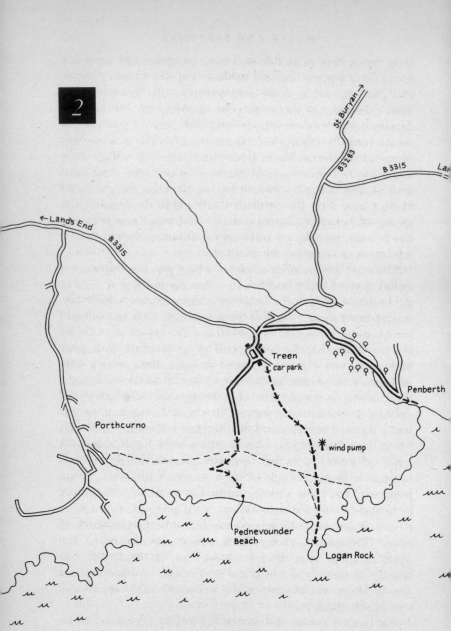

way down it, it is kinder and wiser to walk. The Penberth valley has trees and daffodil fields that give it a rare lushness, and halfway down a gracious (though not ancient) house which boasts among other things the only vineyard in England which produces a saleable *red* wine. I have tasted worse from Morocco (and very much better from a number of places). You catch a glimpse of the house through a gatehouse which spans the stream. Below this is the last possible place to leave and turn a car, then a bridge, and you emerge into the cove itself with its granite slipway and a group of fishermen's cottages. For Penberth is a working cove, with boats and a fishermen's co-operative and not an ice-cream to be had in the place. It is not a spot for bathing, but there are places among the rocks on either arm of the cove where you can sit and stare.

Harder to find, on the opposite coast, is the Trevail walk, whose prize is the possibility of spotting seals. You begin with the St Ives to Zennor road (B3306) and leave your car on the rising slopes of Trendrine Hill within sight of the Eagle's Nest: don't try to put it down a side lane – there is no room, and you risk an argument with a piece of farm machinery. The lane to Trevail comes off at the foot of the hill in the St Ives direction. First it passes a farm called Wicca, goes due north to Trevail Farm, and then right past a fairytale cottage, down to Trevail Mill. This is an enchanted place, but the owner deserves to be left in peace and our way lies over a stone stile on the left, just before we reach the mill. A sign indicates 'To River Cove', and in Cornwall anything more permanent than a trickle is a river.

It is the kind of path you can imagine smugglers staggering up by moonlight, each with a cask on his shoulder. The branches close in over your head, the stream rushes and glitters among the bushes, and you wonder where you are going. The important principle is to keep up to the left, which eventually will join you on to the Coastal Path. Follow this to the left, westwards, and you will soon find yourself over-looking a group of rocks – The Carracks – where the seals gather to watch the trippers who come out in boatloads from St Ives. Without too much difficulty you can find a zigzag

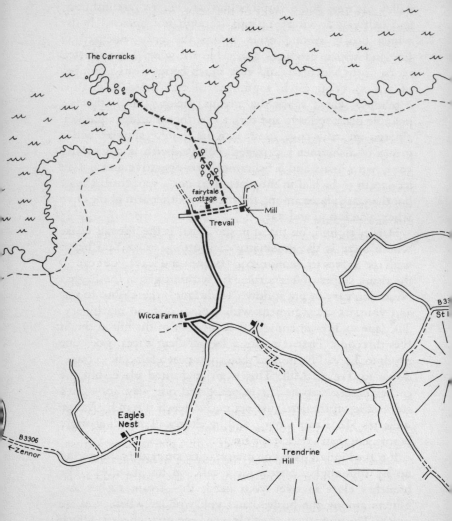

The Carracks

fairytale
cottage

Mill

Trevail

Wicca Farm

B33
St I

Eagle's
Nest

B3306
← Zennor

Trendrine
Hill

Towedna

3

path down the cliff face that will bring you to sea-level and
the chance of a closer sight of the seals. And there are pools
you can bathe in, or trap inedible scurrying crabs.

The third walk I would recommend is more of a pilgrimage, and though not an exacting one it just might bring you
some supernatural benefit. It is the walk to the Well of St
Madron or Maddern.

The Celts recognized springs and wells to be nipples of the
Earth Mother. The Church, needing Holy Water for baptism,
wisely appropriated them. There is hardly a saint in Cornwall
that does not have his own, and many of them have special
properties to commend them. St Nun's Well, at Altarnun,
was said to cure insanity; St Uny's to treat intestinal disease;
while baptism in the waters of St Ruth's, at Redruth, was a
guarantee against death by hanging. Gulval Well answered
questions about absent friends by gushing clear if they were
well, or turning muddy if they were dead. St Ludgvan's Well
was originally multi-purpose, curing dumbness and poor
eyesight as well as keeping the hangman at bay: but then the
Devil spat in it, making it ineffectual against anything but
hanging by a common hempen noose. A peer christened in it
was not immune to the silken cord.

St Maddern's Well must have been highly effective in its
day, for it has a string of seventeenth- and eighteenth-century
credits for curing cripples, and to this day people drop coins
in it and wish, or attach pieces of rag to the nearby bushes, as
they do as far apart as Ireland and Pakistan as notices of
petition. According to one account, girls used to fix two
inch-long pieces of straw together with a pin, making a cross,
and then drop it into the well: the number of bubbles rising to
the surface told them how many years they must wait to be
married.

To visit the Well today, first obtain a pair of gumboots. If
you come by car, you take the turning off the Madron to
Morvah road which is signposted: Wishing Well ½ Bos-
warthen ¾. A little way down this lane you come to a further
sign pointing to the right, saying Madron Wishing Well.
There you park your car, climb a stone stile and walk along a
path between blackthorns sprayed with grey-green lichen.

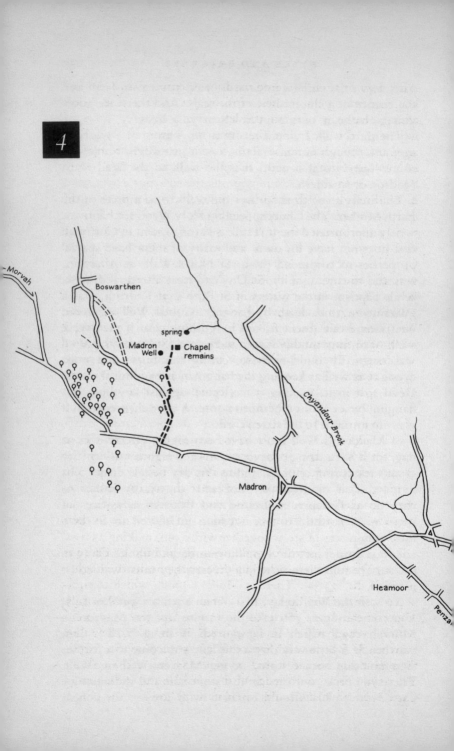

After two or three hundred yards, you curve to the left and keep on among the bushes, crossing yet another stile. Soon after, there is a path to the left with a battered tin sign indicating the well; but first visit the baptistry, which is another fifty yards ahead. It is a small roofless cell, about twelve feet by eight, with the altar slab at one end, stone benches along the wall, and opposite the entrance a baptismal niche through which the water flows live – in a wet season and when nobody has been tampering with it – to form a pool, rather than a font. It is still used for baptisms, usually at mid-summer, and I cannot think of a better place for a Christian soul to be made regenerate and born anew of water, with the minimum of churchly confinement. Over the wall, you can look north towards Carfury and Ding Dong.

Now you go back again to where the path leads off to the Well, deep in the thickets. This is Wellington boot country, a pilgrimage through the Slough of Despond or the swamps of Mississippi. The Well, when you get there, consists of a small chasm roughly lined with stones into which two little streams piddle. The rags on the nearby bushes give it a gypsy air, though one of them I examined turned out to be a bill for £5.60 at the Newlyn Meadery. There was also a cross farmer who relied on the Well to feed his cattle troughs, and whose water had been cut off by boys who had been pulling the stonework apart to get at the coins dropped in by visitors. Up to 1830, when Madron was the mother church for Penzance, the Penzance water supply came from this well, allowing the well-to-do the distinction of hot and cold holy water in their bathrooms.

The peninsula is full of walking-goals like these. There is Zennor Quoit, to be reached up the track opposite the Eagle's Nest on the B3306. There is Mulfra Quoit, which is sign-posted off the Ding Dong and Trythall Lane, above Newmill. There is the stone circle of Boscawen-Un (or Boscawen-Noon), very hard to find swamped in bracken on a line between St Buryan and Sancreed. My own favourite circle, though it has been restored, is generally referred to as the Tregeseal Circle, at the edge of the moorland to the south of Carn Kenidjack. I should reach it by following the rough

track that crosses the B3318, visiting first the battleship-like
Carn itself (which has a reputation for being haunted), spying
out the circle from a distance and then following the moorland paths first west and then south. On these moors it is
always best to follow what paths there are and go the long
way round, rather than wade through the gorse and brambles
along what appears to be the shortest distance between two
points. On the south-eastern slopes of the Carn, marked only
on the largest-scale maps, is a row of holed stones, very
mysterious. The holes are much smaller than the Men-an-Tol
and do nothing to clear up the riddle of their purpose. Just
before visiting them for the first time, I had been in Guernsey
where there are at least two standing stones which have been
endowed with female heads and breasts: a warning against
any assumption that standing stones must necessarily be male
and phallic.

Stone is so essential to this landscape that you may wish to
make a more scientific approach. I am no geologist, but as I
understand it the Penwith peninsula is a dome of granite
which has been pushed up through the original 'country
rocks' of slate, lava and diabase or dolerate types, so that you
get granite in the centre of the peninsula and a thin, incom-
plete fringe of less noble rock around the edges. Indeed, so
much of the fringe has been washed and worn away that it is
only noticeable at points along the north coast and behind
Penzance. What makes the geologist's mouth water is a spot
where granite and country rock meet.

The most easily accessible point is beside Cape Cornwall,
an ideal view for the incapacitated, for you can drive your car
– carefully – right out to the vantage point high up on the
cliffs. At the Tregeseal crossroads on the B3306, at the foot of
the hill that leads to St Just, you take a narrow, unpromising
lane westwards towards the sea. This climbs the side of the
valley and leads up to some empty mine craters where you
can safely park, to look out on the back of the Cape itself and
on a complex of mine ruins that look as old as the Roman
Forum.

But I shall assume you are more active and direct you to the
coastal path between the Gurnard's Head and Bosigran Castle

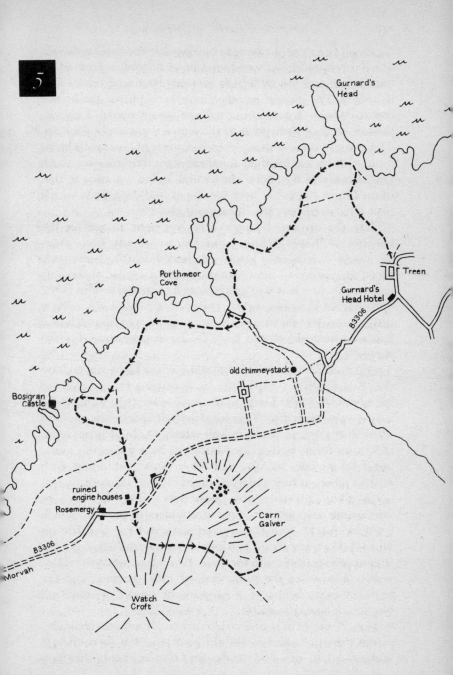

(again off the 3306). Leave your car outside the hotel and walk down through the battered little hamlet behind it. Fork left at the bottom and follow a path between two wire fences into the fields. The general principle now is to pursue the line of the telephone wires going to the coastguards' lookout, though keeping somewhat to the left of them and higher up. This brings you to a strange, end-on view of Gurnard's Head itself – which was fortified about the second century B.C. with ramparts across the neck. The natural design is similar to that of the Logan Rock, but here we do not find the granite which makes the southern castle so magnificent.

Here the original country rock has been altered by the pushing of fiery granite from below. It has been *meta-morphosed* – changed – into hard, dark hornfels, sometimes called greenstone in these parts, though you only observe its greenness when it is wet and polished by the sea. This is the bull-head of the cape, where the rock is hardest. Its neck is softer, more like the original slate, which is why so much of it has been washed away to leave the headland jutting into the waves.

You go left now, over the shoulder of the Cape and pick up the coastal path at a gap in the stone hedge a few yards from the edge of the cliff. The path lies outside the field wall, which is an invaluable index of geology in itself. For as the rocks in the field change, so does the wall which was built from them: at first uniform, fine-grained hornfels, then pieces of granite begin to intrude, looking like an uncooked pudding with distinct pieces of fruit and suet stirred into the mixture.

Rounding a corner you look down into the cove of Porthmeor. It is full of rounded boulders of granite, which contrast clearly with the layered slate and the hornfels on which you are standing. You curve down to the left, cross the stream and scramble into the cove. If you look up to the right, you will now see the two types of rock meeting; and the tumbled mass below is a mixture of brown granite and blue-black hornfels or slate.

The granite here is of a coarse grain. 'Grain', incidentally, means 'texture' and you should be careful not to confuse it with the 'grain' of wood. Rocks *have* similar lines of direction in them, but this is called 'dip'. Where they dip gently, as they do now to the west, you get gently sloping cliffs. Where the dip has been tilted to the near-vertical, you get a hard resisting cliff face.

The ingredients of the granite pudding are variable. The suety white pieces are felspar. The black, glistening particles are mica, which appear like little books with pages. There are fragments of clear quartz (not, alas, diamonds). And there are sometimes black crystalline threads of tourmaline, which you will find together with quartz in a black-and-white granite.

If you have had enough, you can now climb back up the valley, keeping to the fields to the right of the stream. At the top is an old chimney-stack, and below it to the left the ruins of a water-mill that drove the tin-stamps – a primitive ore-crushing plant that served the little mines in the moors above. To get back to the road, and the easy way to your car at the Gurnard's Head hotel, keep on through the fields to the right of the chimney-stack.

Bolder spirits and stronger legs will want to follow the coastal path on to the west, however, and it is a pleasant walk, though exposed if the wind and waves are fetching all the way from America. You will hardly recognize the cliff-castle of Bosigran at first, for it is flat topped and its eastern flanks slope quite gently. It is only when you step onto it and look down over the western edge that you catch your breath and back hastily away in horror. There, dangling below you on ropes, with their bright-coloured helmets, are the rock-climbers. The wrinkled sea beneath them crawls; and every now and then, one falls.

Climbers occasionally scramble up the suicidal neck of the Gurnard's Head, too. You may find it marked on your map as 'Treen (or Treryn) Dinas', the same name that is used confusingly for the Logan Rock. Treryn means 'Farm on the hillside', which is the name for both neighbouring hamlets; but Dinas is the old Cornish for 'Cliff castle', making the name Castel-an-Dinas mean nothing more than 'Castle castle', yet another sad token of how the Cornish forgot the sense of their own language.

From Bosigran you will probably feel like heading back for

the road, which lies behind the two ruined engine-houses that you can see inland. But if you still have energy to spare you might complete this geological tour by crossing over the road, taking the track that lies in the valley between the hills of Watch Croft and Carn Galver and turning left at the top to explore the superstructure of blocks and cheeses and pancakes. There is no vulgar country rock here; this is all granite, first softened underground by the acid soil, then exposed, then washed and blasted by the wind and rain and sometimes vandalized by the local inhabitants in search of easy-to-find building materials.

Stand on the summit, look down and imagine the gigantic forces that have gone into the making of all this. Long before the sea started gnawing at it, think of the subterranean pressures that could force up billions of tons, the heat that produced rock like toffee, the squeezing that forced one rock into another, that converted one kind into another, that drove jets of mineralized gases through veins and cracks, and the stresses set up when it all cooled down again, twisting and cracking. The earth in which the Cornishman plants his broccoli is a thin veneer.

If you wander through Penwith the rocks can speak to you of all their struggles and sufferings. Sylvia, who was a painter and printmaker long before she took up photography, became fascinated by their grain and dip, as she did by countless abstract details within the more obviously picturesque scenes – by a chain across the sand, a tin can stuck on a twig, a pattern of pebbles, the rhythms of a stone hedge. So do not look only for the grand views; for such miniatures have as much to say about the place as a desolate moor or a grand cliff. Standing on my window-ledge in London, I have two large rounded pebbles, picked up in one of the coves, which are a source of extraordinary calm to me.

This raises the last dilemma: is it right to threaten the ancient calm and remoteness of Penwith by displaying it like this, by giving the game away? Should anyone who loves it help to open it up to still more tourism?

I must confess that I have held a few things back, out of selfishness and out of respect for others. But against my

doubts, I balance other considerations. Penwith, like Cornwall as a whole, has had a raw deal from government after
government where development aid is concerned: its unemployment figures are a scandal, and if it had a large labour-
intensive industry and powerful trade unions at work, no
doubt money would have been directed its way freely as it has
been to the North of England. Even its farming and fishing
are at the mercy of bigger battalions, and its holiday trade is at
the mercy of the sun and of soaring travel costs. It seems to
me no service to the people of Penwith to rejoice when
visitors are kept away. Anything we may do to convince
them that this is a place worth saving their petrol for, or
worth walking and bicycling over, seems to me doubly
justified. It helps the Cornish make a living and it enriches the
visitor with experiences that can last (as they have done for
me) a lifetime. I and my family are by no means the only ones
to have been enriched like this; in a little-known sketch
Virginia Woolf wrote:

'In retrospect, probably nothing that we had as children was quite so
important to us as our summer in Cornwall. To go away to the end
of England; to have that bay, that sea, and the Mount: Clodgy and
Halsetown Bog; Carbis Bay; Lelant; Zennor; Trevail, the Gurnard's Head; to hear the waves breaking that first night behind the
yellow blind . . . I could fill pages remembering one thing after
another that made the summer at St Ives the best beginning to a life
conceivable. When they took Talland House (in St Ives), my father
and mother gave me, at any rate, something I think invaluable.
Suppose I had only Surrey or Sussex or the Isle of Wight to think
about when I think about my childhood.'

An Appendix of Islands

On a clear day from the cliffs of Penwith, between Zennor and Land's End, you can see islands on the horizon. They are almost thirty miles away to the southwest and by rights another country, almost another book. The trouble is, it would be a slim volume and might miss getting read altogether, for the Isles of Scilly, romantic though they are, are almost devoid of folklore and pretty thin on history.

Why is an interesting question. Helicoptering down on a sunny spring morning, with the waters below every shade of turquoise, sapphire and jade, you might think they were full of fairy tales. But they aren't; and I think the reason is that they simply have not got the continuity of Cornwall. Indeed, they are actually governed by something called the Council of the Isles and, as the maps point out, are not part of Cornwall county at all.

Spread over an area about eight miles by eight there are five inhabited islands, none of them worth the expense of a motor car (though lamentably there are a few), and dozens of rocky lumps and bumps with names but no inhabitants. You are only twenty minutes from the mainland by air or two and a half hours by boat. But the divorce is more complete than you expect. Up to the present century the islands were an unreliable destination, just too far and too bleak for the mainland Cornish to bother with. The inhabitants of Scilly, for their part, tended to have their own private reasons for being there. Either they were garrison troops or they were pirates, wreckers, smugglers or criminals in flight from the law. Otherwise there was nothing that could be done on Scilly that could not be better done elsewhere. Contrary to legend, copper and tin are not among the treasures of the place, and Scillonians are never miners. Goodness knows, mainland Cornwall was a hard enough country. But Scilly, though mild, was too windswept for corn and too cut off from the markets of the mainland to make more than tolerable farmsteading. At some point in the Dark Ages it seems to have become *in*tolerable, and the original population scrambled ashore.

It is likely for this reason that the Cornish language died out in Scilly before it did in Penwith; for although Scilly has plenty of Cornish place names they are often distorted into pidgin English. The characteristic Scillonian family names have nothing of Tre-, Pol- and Pen- about them (Hicks is typical), and they seem to have arrived from Kent or Shropshire in the eighteenth or nineteenth centuries.

If there were once Cornishmen living on Scilly – and there must have been to give so many traces of Cornish to the landscape – then as I say there must have been some point at which they got up and moved out, leaving the place to a succession of immigrants. My guess is that that point came when some major flooding of the islands (or island) obliged a majority of the population to leave for the mainland. I would plump for a date around A.D. 500, but a century or two earlier or later might answer. At any rate it is the origin of the Lost Land of Lyonesse legend. There was not a continuous flooding from Mount's Bay to Scilly, with Arthur's knights struggling ashore in the Isles of the Blest, leaving dozens of parish churches and their belfries tolling beneath the waves, but there was a great flooding at either end, and lesser advances of the sea since. Certainly the face of Scilly has changed considerably in the last two thousand years.

Professor Charles Thomas, who is the undoubted expert on the subject, believes that once upon a time Scilly consisted of one big island comprising all today's inhabited isles except St Agnes', and it is easy enough, at low tides, to see the logic of this. One can still see the tops of field walls on the sandbanks, and there are folk-memories of walkable causeways joining the islands together in near-living memory – for example there was said to be a man living in 1935 who had walked from St Mary's to St Martin's on secret causeways;

while the walk from Tresco to Bryher and Bryher to Samson is still practicable on the low spring tides today.

A Greater Scilly, say in Roman times, would not have been a thriving agricultural community any more than mainland Penwith was. People have always come to the extreme southwest for other reasons than the crops, and in the case of Scilly their reason was largely numinous. The oldest things on the islands are the tombs that crown the highlands and hills. There are far more than could have been accounted for by the local population – perhaps about five hundred in various states of dilapidation – so that one gets the picture of a mysterious land of the dead, on the edge of the known world, to which the great chieftains of west Cornwall were brought for burial. In one particular site, the crest of Samson south hill, the graves are so tightly packed together that one gets the impression of a Hill of the Kings, a cherished royal burial ground. And one should not think in terms of one man one tomb; many of them contained the ashes of several members of the same tribe.

The holiness seems to have stuck long after this kind of burial went out of fashion. The name 'Scilly' was probably derived from 'Sylina', an Iron Age goddess whom Professor Thomas connects with the deity at Bath ('Sulis'). No matter. We shall never know and there is little point in losing one's hair over it. We do know that the Emperor Maximus exiled two heretical bishops to 'insula Sylina' in A.D. 381, and the position just about fits. Besides being far away from susceptible congregations, Scilly must have seemed about the end of the known religious world – as far as one could go without actually being liquidated.

That it was a place of visitation, of pilgrimage even, is shown by excavations carried out as recently as the 1960s on the small, now uninhabited island of Nornour. Archaeologists working here have uncovered quantities of brooches and knick-knacks such as would suggest either a small factory or a shop dealing in souvenirs; in fact one might call Nornour one of the earliest sources of tourist junk in the British Isles.

The work dates from the first century to the fourth A.D., which makes it Celtic pre-Christian or loosely under Roman auspices. It is worth noting that the materials used were by no means local (as I've said, there was no tin or copper let alone gold on Scilly) so it was not a question of exploiting what was to hand. People wanted a Nornour brooch because of where it came from and because of the magical qualities that the provenance supplied. In particular they wanted a souvenir of having been there or a votive offering for some shrine near by. Professor Thomas suggests there may have been a sacred beacon – a kind of primitive lighthouse – burning on Scilly, and that the likeliest place for it was the site of the modern dark-mark on St Martin's. But no one has come up with a heap of ashes to prove it.

Nornour brings us within striking distance of the Christian era; indeed it could be within it, because there is no doubt that Christianity came to the British Isles with the Romans, well before St Augustine arrived in A.D. 597. But it does not seem likely that the faith spread as far as Cornwall in that first attempt. Again, it was there ahead of Augustine, maybe as early as A.D. 400 though more likely well into the 500s; the question is, where did it come from? I think the answer is from Ireland and Wales, and that it first set foot on the Cornish mainland in the Hayle estuary.

But we must not forget the exiled bishops in the Scillies: their date (and there is nothing mythical about it) is 381, and the fact that they were exiled to Scilly suggests that there was already a Christian presence there to restrain them.

In fact the bishops were Priscillians (a kind of Manichaean Dualists, devoted to apocryphal scriptures) and although Priscillian himself suffered the ignominy of beheading, the movement underwent a revival following the fall of the Emperor Maximus and it is quite possible that our two bishops were restored to favour. The point is that they came from Spain, where Priscillianism was all the rage, and it is possible that Scilly got its Christianity from that direction, not from Britain or Ireland. If so, it follows that there were Christian holy men in the islands before there were any in Penwith, though they may have been holy men of a fierce and unorthodox kind.

But it is no good pretending that Scilly was to become a

notable centre of devotion or theology. There are no such buildings, either of the massive Latin variety or the cellular Celtic type. The Scillonian Church consisted of small island chapels serving peasant communities, which failed to grow as the Middle Ages progressed – as those on the mainland did – and did not keep the name of their saintly founders after the Cornish custom. On the contrary, the chapel names which have come down to us are all out of the Roman calendar – St Mary, St Martin, St Agnes, St Nicholas (Tresco), St Helen.

But they got these names fairly late, in the course of the Norman conquest when the last traces of the Celtic Church were being removed and Cornwall was being ruled ecclesiastically from Tavistock. In 1120 Scilly had a Benedictine priory on Tresco under a monk known as Turod. In those days St Martin's was still known by the Celtic name of Nutho, and St Helen's was called *St Elidius*, a name of the Celtic, not Roman, calendar.

This is interesting, because St Elidius was evidently sufficiently respected to be worthy of preservation. The monks of Tavistock restored his cell and built a special shrine with a marble lid which bears all the signs, to this day, of being the founder's tomb. In a small way it may have been a place of pilgrimage until about the end of the fifteenth century. It is tempting to link it with the tourist junk on Nornour, though this is two miles away on another island.

In any case there is the figure of St Elidius to be accounted for. For a start, he is not to be confused – though he easily is – with a French saint called Eligius or Eloi of about the same period in the early seventh century. Elidius or Eliud is better known in his native Wales as St Teilo, and he was an associate of the Breton St Samson, who also has Scillonian connections. But there is no suggestion that Teilo–Elidius lived in Scilly, for his tomb is in Llandaff cathedral and was opened in the eighteenth century and found to contain a genuine bishop. So although a dedication to the Pembrokeshire saint is not too hard to explain, it is not he who is buried on St Helen's island and the local people should have known it. If there is a candidate, he is an anonymous one.

One is tempted by a story in the Icelandic saga of one

Snorri Sturluson. It relates how the redoubtable Olaf Trygg-vason arrives one day in the island of 'Syllingar' and hears of a holy man living there with remarkable powers. At first Olaf sends a servant dressed in his costume to test the saint; but the sage sees through the deception and insists on confronting Tryggvason in person. Being confronted, he forecasts that on returning to his boat Tryggvason will be treacherously stabbed, but will recover on the seventh day and live to see the error of his sins.

It all comes true. Olaf is baptized and becomes a recruiting officer for the Christian faith, taking it with him back to Scandinavia and several monks as well. Well, it may be true and it may not, and anyway Scilly may not be 'Syllingar'. All one can be sure of is that something holy happened on St Helen's island and that it is really the only Christian holy place of any reputation in the islands.

What is more, you can still visit it. St Helen's being uninhabited, is not on the daily rota of islands served by the ferries, but if the weather is calm and a boat is going between St Martin and Old Grimsby on the east coast of Tresco, you may be able to beg a landing on it. You will be landed on a sand-spit to the south of the island. Make for the shore line, and when you strike it turn right for the ruined chapel, which is just a little way inland on the slope of the hill. It is well worth seeing, with the saint's beehive cell and the chapel with the positions of the altar and shrine clear to see. If you go left on striking the shore line you come to a much more recent nineteenth-century ruin which was the island pest-house where incoming sailors with undesirable diseases were kept in quarantine.

St Helen's is almost inhabitable today, though it is fearfully prickly and overgrown. I guess the main objection must always have been shortage of water, for I have not been able to find any there, and only a miserable trickle on that other tempting candidate for habitation, Samson.

It probably didn't matter much in Norman times, for St Elidius could quite easily be reached on foot from Tresco, where there was water and the settlement of monks from Tavistock. They seem to have been the only civilized things about the place during most of the Middle Ages; for although Edward I established a lord of sorts on St Mary's (the main island) in 1306, the lord came to the conclusion that he was better off siding with the local wreckers and pirates than making a lonely stand for law and order. There were times when you might have thought Scilly had fallen into foreign hands, so numerous were French and Spanish privateers in the anchorage. With the dissolution of the priory, the islands became little more than a haven for raiders and runaways.

The age of the Spanish Armada made Scillonian anarchy intolerable, and Elizabeth I was the woman to put a stop to it. In 1571 she granted a Crown lease of the islands – which lasted till 1831 – to Francis Godolphin, for £10 a year. But it was no idle curio, for Elizabeth required the building on St Mary's of a small castle – known as Star Castle from its shape – to act as a lookout and guardian of the anchorage. It was to have a lieutenant, 3 gunners and 26 footsoldiers in the summer – only 10 soldiers in winter, as a gesture of Elizabethan economy. It had 6 cannon and a stock of muskets and pikes and it was assumed that locally engaged help would be available in time of emergency.

The castle was rushed up in a matter of months, Godolphin reporting dutifully to Lord Burghley: 'Seldom has so much been performed at such small charge and with so few hands in so short a time.' As is common in this part of the world, the building was done with second-hand stones, including almost certainly the remains of ancient tombs, and the bill came to £450.

The Spaniards were not the only peril to be run in the western approaches, for in the early seventeenth century Cornwall was harried surprisingly closely by the Turks or Barbary corsairs from Morocco. In 1636 Sir Francis Godolphin was taken captive by them while on his way to the Scillies and never seen again. It is likely that he finished his days as a galley slave in a Moorish ship, as many Cornish fishermen did unless they were ransomed.

The Civil Wars were probably the liveliest period of Scillonian history, if not the most fortunate. Like most of the West Country, Scilly sided with the King and Star Castle was probably the last royalist stronghold in the kingdom. A parliamentary fleet which tried to reduce it by bombardment was scattered by storm, though the royalists were then reduced to supporting themselves by piracy.

The next people to turn up were the Dutch under Van Tromp, who went to the length of declaring war on the Scilly Isles, a condition which actually survived to the 1980s, when it was terminated with much ceremony and more television coverage than the islands had ever enjoyed before. Tromp teamed up with the parliamentarians, who began by taking Tresco after a somewhat farcical night landing which involved invading the wrong island. Still, there was a brisk fight and a week later, following a bombardment by the Dutch fleet, St Mary's was taken with a garrison of fifteen hundred men, short of supplies and without hope of relief. Generously, they were allowed to go provided they scattered abroad. The Godolphins were even permitted to keep the tenancy of the islands, on the grounds that they at least knew the outlandish place and nobody on the side of parliament did or wanted to.

The parliamentary forces, in the light of their own successful invasion, constructed the pretty little castle that dominates the anchorage between Tresco and Bryher. But Cromwell soon neglected it. By 1658 the governor of the islands was complaining that his gunnery was useless because the powder was damp and the ammunition down to two rounds per gun – a complaint that seems to have had no effect at all. On the Restoration the islands returned to royalism without a shot and Star Castle became a political prison for downfallen Cromwellians.

It perked up again in the mid-eighteenth century, when the Block House was built to guard the eastern anchorage at Tresco, and again in the Napoleonic Wars. Islanders were required to hold themselves available for defence, and were forbidden to absent themselves to the mainland without permission of the commanding officer. But there was much less building of fortifications and batteries than one might have supposed. The fact is, Scilly is very tricky sailing and has never been a good fleet anchorage. Alien ships have always given the rocks and islands a wide berth if they could. For men-of-war with a deep draught the inviting haven of Crow Sound could turn into a death trap. In fact, the bigger ships became, the safer Star Castle was. The easiest way to protect Scilly was to withdraw the pilots and leave the enemy to wreck himself. And in fact most of Scilly's many wrecks were on the outer rocks and ledges, not on her inner defences.

For centuries the permanent population of Scilly seems to have varied between 1,500 and 2,500 souls. The capital, Hugh Town on St Mary's, kept its sixteenth-century reputation of being 'a poor town, sore defaced and worn'. Until the last century or so the problem was to find a cash crop for the islands. In the mid-seventeenth century kelp-burning – the production of seaweed ash for rendering into iodine – was introduced from Brittany, but it provided a miserable living. Then there was smuggling and wrecking, knitting, early potato growing, lobster potting – largely for the knowing French – but really nothing worked until the arrival of the railway in Penzance and the happy coincidence of the daffodils in winter and the tourists in spring, summer and autumn.

At this point – about 1834 on the calendar – it is time to introduce the illustrious name of Augustus Smith, without whom Scilly would not be what it is today, or has been for the past century and a half.

Smith had already made a reputation for himself at Berkhamsted in Hertfordshire, as a champion of the people. When Lord Brownlow attempted to enclose Berkhamsted Common as part of the Ashridge estate, Smith engaged a trainload of Irish navvies to come down from Euston overnight and pull the railings down. What is more, he got away with it.

But our hero was not altogether averse to private property, for soon afterwards he purchased the Crown lease of the Scilly Isles on their relinquishment by the Godolphin heir, the Earl of Leeds. Smith thus became Lord Proprietor of the Isles, though that rank reverted in due course to the Duchy of Cornwall, and in 1890 a Council of the Isles was set up, consisting of the Lord Proprietor and twenty councillors representing the inhabited islands (only one for Bryher). However, Tresco became the Smith residence and private property, as it remains.

Smith built his home on the site of the priory of the monks of Tavistock, and antiquarians grumble that the baronial hall which he constructed, rather in the style in which his fellow Victorians were building in the Lake District, left little of the ancient ruins. But the glory of Tresco is, of course, the gardens, where Smith realized the fact that one could not enjoy the mildness of the Scillonian climate unless one erected defences against the wind. Thus Tresco has an appearance foreign to all the other islands, of black branches of pines and cypresses against the skyline, and a hint of wolves in the forest. For it is the only island to boast anything in the way of woodland, thanks to the passion of Augustus Smith – and even more his successor – for planting wind-breaks.

On the southward-facing slope of the lower end of Tresco, Smith constructed a series of terraces joined by steps. On these he grew a great variety of semi-tropical plants, many of them recently introduced from Australia and New Zealand and grown out of doors in the British Isles for the first time. Today one is struck by the enormous height of the palms and eucalyptuses, the bamboos and yuccas, and by the generosity with which things like camellias and fuchsias bloom, not to mention unheard-of oddities like proteas and banksias. When the gardens were completed in about 1855 there were extensive glasshouses, too. But fuel and labour were cheaper in those days, and the seventeen acres of formal planting were more rigidly disciplined than they are today.

Even so, I don't think we should put Augustus Smith's gardening before his social engineering, for he took Scilly by the scruff of the neck and pushed it, in some ways, into the twentieth century before the twentieth century had arrived. The islands were his, and anyone who lived there had to live the Smith way. At the time many thought it was capricious and tyrannical, but in fact it was eminently practical.

For example, Smith insisted that land on the islands should cease to be divided between all the surviving sons and should go strictly to the eldest. The rest could emigrate, which was actually best for all of them. He also introduced compulsory schooling for island children long before the mainland had it, and numerous forms of public works. Nearly all the jetties which play so important a part in island comings and goings are of Augustus Smith origin.

He applied himself, too, to the problem of a money-earning occupation for the islands, and very nearly solved it. Smith's answer was small boat construction, from the celebrated Scillonian pilot gigs which are still used for racing to sailing barges of a hundred tons or more. By 1850 he had five boatyards on St Mary's turning out about ten small boats a year each.

Smith's least popular move was the evacuation of Samson, which took place in 1855. The island was said to have been inhabited by two staunchly Baptist families called the Woodcocks and the Webbers who, when Smith arrived on Scilly, numbered some thirty souls in half a dozen cottages, and those stoutly built. But by 1850 they were down to ten and five years later there remained only a single woman named Ann Webber (who of course had the reputation of being a witch).

Samson looks romantic and there are still free spirits who try living there in the ruins, under a few sheets of plastic, in the summer season. But in fact it is a bleak place. The few level fields seem to have been engulfed by the sea and drenched with sand long ago, and the one trickle of fresh water would hardly suit modern needs. The island still has some of the best built stone hedges on Scilly, and a flock of sooty black rabbits scampers for cover as you land; but outside the ruined cottages the heaps of limpet shells – bottom of the barrel for the poor – tell the story of Samson's last descent into poverty. A few sheep and cattle were left to graze on the island, then nothing. People are always applying to go and live there, but it is a melancholy place. Best satisfy yourself with a day trip, by arrangement with one of the boatmen. He will put you down at the foot of the north hill and you can follow the contour of the island up and down to its neck, and then up again to the south hill where the best ruins and tombs are. Then you will have to retrace your steps to the landing; Samson requires more walking than you might at first think.

Augustus Smith is said to have been cursed by Ann Webber

for evicting her from her desert island, and he got a reputation for heartlessness for it; but really he did her a favour. Nor was the curse very effective, for Smith lived until 1872, a rule of thirty-eight years. The Tresco guide-book describes a regular royal family in the Smith line since then, for Augustus was succeeded by his nephew (who began as Algernon Smith Dorrien Smith, but was allowed to shorten it to Dorrien-Smith) and he by his son the major, and by *his* son the commander, and he by the present proprietor, Mr Robert Dorrien-Smith. All have taken the family trust extremely seriously and worked hard at it, particularly the gardens. The present incumbent has tried to make them pay their way, shipping packaged plants to the mainland as well as selling pots at the souvenir shop, and he has converted nearly forty of his properties into holiday flats and time-share cottages. You might think the latter move hard on would-be islanders, but the argument is that forty more families without work on Tresco have made way for the tourist money. Certainly the cottages are enchanting, and you can buy all the supplies you need on the island. Though it's not cheap it makes a blissful holiday and I say good luck to the Dorrien-Smiths and their efforts to survive.

But it is the second in line, Algernon, who deserves the thanks of the wider Scillies, for it was he who saw the possibilities of the daffodil trade. It is said that he found them growing wild in the priory gardens, where they had been tended by the monks as Lenten Lilies. But it is also said that the bulbs were shovelled out of the hold of a Dutch coaster as some sort of inferior onions. Be that as it may, the flowers made their first momentous trip to Covent Garden in a hat-box in 1881 and have never looked back. They probably reached London as swiftly a hundred years ago as they do today, when something like 800 tons of flowers in the year are sent to market.

It's little use, though, going to see the flower fields in the London spring. January is the height of the season – goodness knows, it may be earlier if the greenhouse effect comes into play – and most of the flowers are picked in bud. Still, if you go in February you may find mild weather and enough

left-over flowers in the little fields to give you an idea of what
a full show must be like; and there are plenty of runaways in
the hedges and waysides.

I would not like it thought that I regard Scilly as a mere day
or weekend trip. It is much more, especially for children of –
say – from five to eleven, for whom it is a real imagination-
stretcher. Apart from anything else, you can rampage all day
and not meet a motor-car, unless you are foolish enough to
stay on St Mary's.

I haven't much to say for St Mary's; nothing against it
either. It's the sort of place one needs for shopping and
banking and maybe the chemist once a week, and there are
two or three distinguished tombs and Star Castle to see. But
there is something ever so slightly – well – suburban about it,
which the other islands would not touch. It has a folk
museum which looks terribly like the usual junky Cornish
farmyard, and an alleged Nature Trail which is a path
through a bog labelled 'Nature Trail'. It starts at Holy Vale,
which is not nearly as pretty as its name suggests.

There is also on St Mary's a joy for the ecologically minded
in the shape of a colossal windmill to generate electricity, a
task which it carries out experimentally since Scilly now gets
its current by cable from the mainland. Since the 1950s it has
also imported another modernism, the curse of income tax,
which everyone swore would be the death of life on the
islands, but somehow it hasn't.

Perhaps the real purpose of St Mary's is to absorb the shock
of the day trippers and leave the serious visitors to get on with
the off-islands undisturbed. Of these there are four: St
Martin's, St Agnes', Tresco and Bryher. I am inclined to say
that the chief pleasure of Scilly is bouncing about from one to
another in the sturdy island ferries whose movements are
chalked up on blackboards at strategic points. One cannot
plan more than a day ahead, because even though the tides can
be forecast the wind and the weather cannot – sometimes you
get no more than half an hour's notice of 'Boat going to
Agnes', and you go with it gratefully, sure of a day's
adventure. The luck of the boats is one of the chief joys of the
islands: all you need is a packet of sandwiches and a can of

beer. It is surprisingly safe, too. Sometimes one peers with alarm at the plunging cockpit, feet below, that one is expected to hurl oneself into, but I have never seen a little old lady upended, nor even a little old gentleman.

Tresco is probably the most visited of the off-islands, not surprisingly. It even has its own helicopter port, neat as the eighteenth hole at a superior golf course, from which you may step straight into the Abbey Gardens and the Valhalla of figureheads from wrecked sailing ships. There are not many man-made objects on the islands worth seeing, but these must carry the prize. Gesturing silently across the lawn at each other, they seem to be reciting whole epics of the ocean, speaking for the invisible ships and crews crowded behind them.

The southern part of Tresco can offer you long stretches of white, deserted sands, and in the season – whenever that is – the big freshwater pool that made the place so desirable for habitation in the early days is a birdwatcher's Heathrow, full of exotic feathered wanderers that have got their flights misrouted or their baggage mislaid. The Dorrien-Smiths provide convenient apartments beside the pool for the birdwatchers, and have built cosy hides among the reedbeds – though whenever I go there there is nothing to be seen but a pair of moorhens and half a dozen mocking geese.

If birds and gardens are not your pleasure, you can easily walk round the northern half of Tresco in an afternoon. To do this you should cut across the waist of the island from New Grimsby village to Old Grimsby – a quiet little place with a rather expensive new hotel, though in a very pretty position. On the way out of New Grimsby you will pass the New Inn (which is really quite old), a most agreeable pub with excellent food, which makes good use of the pheasants with which this particular island is, unexpectedly, bursting.

By following the northern coast of Tresco anti-clockwise, round to the top, you will come to Piper's Hole, a large cave with a pool in it and a beach on the far side. It is worth taking a torch for this and it is legitimate to give a shudder, for a few years ago an old soldier who felt himself hard done by in the divorce courts did himself to death in the cave and was found floating in the pool.

If I were you I would give it a miss and walk round to the ruins of King Charles's castle and the Cromwellian castle that succeeded it; here you get a charming view of the anchorage between Tresco and Bryher and the raging seas on the far side of the latter. You will want to go into Cromwell's Castle and explore it; or rather you will if you are of an age to bring Treasure Island to life. Across the water is the suggestively named Hangman's Island, and somebody keeps its memory green by maintaining a gibbet in order at its summit.

Thus in twenty minutes or so you may come back to New Grimsby where the boat usually (but not always) picks you up, and on a fine day a most enjoyable ramble it is. It is sometimes possible to buy a lobster in New Grimsby, though they are never cheap anywhere these days. Many years ago – let us say fifty-five – crabs were sixpence each on Scilly, for giant size, and pilchards were dragged on to the beach in seine nets.

The best of the islands for my money is Bryher, which you may be able to combine with a visit to Tresco, for it is just a few hundred yards across the anchorage between them and, as I say, there are times when you can walk between them on dry sand.

The word for Bryher is *wild*. It has none of the earnestness of Tresco or suburbanity of St Mary's, and there is even something mad and a bit frivolous about it. It is a great source of boats to go to places in, and it is the island for camping on, if that is your idea of comfort. Like all the other off-islands there is a shop where you can buy everything from a frozen chicken to a postcard, though typically it is almost impossible, on these islands, to buy fish unless it is Icelandic fish fingers.

It is easy enough to walk round Bryher in less than a day. The place to spend your time is on the west side, from the pool near the little hotel, up northwards. You will hardly engage in conversation all day, because your head will be full of the roaring of waves, breaking on the miniature islands that populate the seascape of Hell's Bay. It is one of the most exhilarating places that I know, and however calm the beaches of Tresco, Hell's Bay will always be ravening for its dinner, waging pitched battle against the rocks of Bryher.

St Martin's is a long island and a good one for walking on.

The sand is good too. Dare I say it is a bit dull, earnestly dedicated to the growing of bulbs and not much else? Its only claim to glamour is that in 1989 it was the scene of the discovery of Scilly's only trove of gold – a bracelet found on the beach and probably washed from a grave nearby. The subsequent coroner's inquest held in the St Martin's Reading Room was – for the island – the sensation of the century.

The bracelet was found near the site of a rather swish hotel which St Martin's has lately acquired. Some say that Prince Charles, as proprietor and planner in chief of the islands, has betrayed his own standards in letting it be built. I haven't the heart to condemn it – it isn't that much of an eyesore, and it is hard to think of anything else that would bring money to the islands. It is hard, too, to be sure that the money will stay in the islands and all the supplies and labour not be imported.

Last of all comes inevitably St Agnes'; which was always a notable island for seamen, being well placed for getting pilots first on to incoming shipping. There is a great revival of the sport of rowing eight-oared Scillonian pilot gigs, and even women's eights pull their way. Agnes is also well placed for watching marine birds, being close to the puffin sanctuary of Annet. But Agnes is painfully small, to my mind, and when you have spent a couple of hours on it you have just about 'done it'. This will annoy people to whom Agnes has something unique – the very end of the very end thereof – but they should be glad that I will be elsewhere, leaving their favourite to themselves.

This is part of the charm of Scilly, that it is varied enough to provide everyone with a favourite island. It is precisely the right size for exploring on foot if you are under twelve or over sixty; and in retrospect you will find that its seas are always blue, its sands always white, and its fields always tossing with golden flowers.

Index